OSPREY COMBAT AIRCRAFT •

LANCASTER SQUADRONS 1942-43

SERIES EDITOR: TONY HOLMES

OSPREY COMBAT AIRCRAFT • 31

LANCASTER SQUADRONS 1942-43

Jon Lake

OSPREY
PUBLISHING

Front Cover
Arguably the most dangerous task of Operation *Chastise* (the famous 'Dams Raid'), flown on 16/17 May 1943, was that allocated to the third wave of Lancasters from No 617 Sqn. Its five aircraft were intended as a 'mobile reserve', having been given the job of attacking whichever targets remained after the first and second waves had dropped their mines. The third wave did not take off until after midnight, and followed the same outbound route as the first wave, over-flying defences that were by now fully alerted. Inevitably, they would then have to make their attacks in the pre-dawn mist, before staggering home as dawn began to break.

The first two aircraft in the wave were shot down en route to the target area. The third aircraft in the final wave (ED918/G, coded AJ-F) was flown by Canadian Flt Sgt K W Brown, and he dropped flares before making several runs against the Sorpe Dam and releasing his *Upkeep* mine at 0314 hrs. He then flew home, surviving heavy flak en route.

The fourth aircraft in the wave (ED886/G, coded AJ-O), flown by Flt Sgt W C Townsend DFM, attacked his target and then revisited the Möhne Dam for a final visual reconnaissance. Townsend flew home at hedge-top height and maximum speed, climbing only to avoid trees, houses and power lines! By the time ED886 ran out between the Dutch islands of Vlieland and Texel, in the direction of the North Sea, the sun had well and truly risen. Sensing an easy kill, German 88 mm flak gunners opened up with everything they had, bouncing shells off the surface of the water at the sea-skimming bomber. However, Townsend and his crew somehow survived unscathed, and eventually made a shaky landing on three engines at Scampton at 0615 hrs, a full 90 minutes after dawn.

The final bomber in the third wave had turned back when its crew became unsure of their position over Germany.

In Iain Wyllie's specially commissioned cover painting, Flt Sgt Townsend is seen hastily turning to starboard in the direction of the open sea after coming under fire from the flak batteries on Texel and Vlieland

First published in Great Britain in 2002 by Osprey Publishing, Midland House, West Way, Botley, Oxford OX2 0PH, UK
443 Park Avenue South, New York, NY 10016, USA
E-mail: info@ospreypublishing.com

ISBN 978 1 84176 313 2

Edited by Tony Holmes
Page design by Tony Truscott
Cover Artwork by Iain Wyllie
Aircraft Profiles by Chris Davey
Scale Drawings by Mark Styling
Typeset in Adobe Garamond, Rockwell and Univers
Origination by Grasmere Digital Imaging, Leeds, UK
Printed and bound in China through Bookbuilders
CIP Data for this publication is available from the British Library

08 09 10 11 12   12 11 10 9 8 7 6 5 4 3

ACKNOWLEDGEMENTS
The Editor wishes to thank Aerospace Publishing, Francis K Mason and Bruce Robertson for the provision of photographs for inclusion in this volume.

EDITOR'S NOTE
To make this best-selling series as authoritative as possible, the Editor would be interested in hearing from any individual who may have relevant photographs, documentation or first-hand accounts relating to the pilots/crews, and their aircraf~ of the various theatres of war. Any material used will be fully credited to its original source. Please write to Tony Holmes at 16 Sandilands, Chipstead, Sevenoaks, Kent, TN13 2SP UK, or via e-mail at: tony.holmes@zen.co.uk-for aviation only

For a catalogue of all Osprey Publishing titles please contact us at:

NORTH AMERICA
Osprey Direct, C/o Random House Distribution Centre, 400 Hahn Road, Westminster, MD 21157
E-mail: info@ospreydirect.com

ALL OTHER REGIONS
Osprey Direct, The Book Service Ltd, Distribution Centre, Colchester Road, Frating Green, Colchester, Essex, CO7 7DW
E-mail: customerservice@ospreypublishing.com

Or visit our website: **www.ospreypublishing.com**

CONTENTS

INTRODUCTION

There is a real difficulty in telling the story of the world's most famous and most successful military aircraft, since there is always the danger of failing to pinpoint the disparities between myth and reality. The more high profile the aircraft, the greater is the danger. And the Lancaster was arguably the most legendary and mythological aircraft to serve with the Royal Air Force during World War 2. In a letter of thanks to A V Roe and Co in December 1945, Sir Arthur Harris described the Lancaster as being the greatest single factor in winning the recent conflict, basing this astonishing claim on the fact that it was responsible for dropping two-thirds of the RAF's bomb tonnage after the beginning of 1942.

The Lancaster formed the backbone of Bomber Command, whose bloody war of attrition against German industry (often misunderstood and sometimes condemned) undeniably laid the foundations of the Allied victory. The Lancaster equipped more squadrons than any other RAF bomber type, and dropped a higher tonnage of bombs. With a tally of ten Victoria Crosses (of the 32 'air' VCs awarded during World War 2), Lancaster aircrew received more VCs than were won by the crews of any other aircraft type. Most observers and analysts at the time, and since, agreed that the aircraft was infinitely better than any of its predecessors or rivals. 'Bomber' Harris himself summarised the conventional wisdom when he baldly stated that;

The seven-man crew of a Lancaster bomber represented the tip of the iceberg in terms of the effort required to place a load of incendiaries and bombs on target, as this propaganda photo attempted to show. Bowser drivers, airframe and engine fitters, armourers, air traffic controllers, parachute packers and Motor Transport drivers are all included in this rather democratic portrait! (*via Bruce Robertson*)

Her own groundcrew watch Lancaster B I DV236 'G-for-George' of No 101 Sqn as she waits for take-off from Ludford Magna, but for the other airmen in the picture this is just another aircraft taking off for just another raid. Just routine, although the odds are stacked against the seven aircrew completing their tour of operations. DV236 was lost on the 15/16 February 1944 raid on Berlin (*via Francis K Mason*)

The crew of this new-looking No 50 Sqn Lancaster B I wait patiently as two carrier pigeons are loaded aboard before they can climb the short entry ladder into the aircraft. This photograph was taken at Skellingthorpe on 15 April 1943, prior to the raid on Stuttgart. ED810 failed to return from its eighth mission (to Oberhausen) on 14/15 June 1943 (*Aerospace Publishing*)

'One Lancaster is to be preferred to four Halifaxes. The Halifax suffers about four times the casualties for a given bomb tonnage. Low ceiling and short range make it an embarrassment when planning attacks with Lancasters.'

In fact, the Lancaster actually suffered a higher loss rate than the Halifax during the daylight raids which predominated at the end of the war, and its crews were more likely to die if their aircraft was shot down. Many also suspect that the Lancaster crews, bombing from higher altitude in greater discomfort, may have been less accurate in delivering their bombs. Finally, although it carried a heavier bombload, the Lancaster was a less useful multi-role aeroplane than the capacious Halifax, and was less well-suited for tropical operations.

But in Arthur Harris's strategic bombing campaign live aircrew in enemy PoW camps were no more useful than the dead, and getting bombs 'bang-on' a pinpoint target was of less concern than saturating what were usually 'area targets'. Nor were the Lancasters' abilities in what Harris saw as 'secondary' roles and theatres of any great concern. The fact that the average Lancaster delivered 154 tons of bombs in its 27.2 sortie life, and could reach beyond Berlin, made it more useful than a shorter-range Halifax averaging only 100 tons. As a result, Lancasters dropped 608,612 tons of bombs out of a Bomber Command total of 955,044.

With these advantages being enjoyed by an aircraft which was also cheaper to produce, it was inevitable that the Lancaster would be built in larger numbers than any other bomber, and would bear the brunt of the bombing campaign. They were despatched on 156,192 operational sorties during the war, and some 3836 were lost. These sorties included 107,085 on raids against Germany (23,204 of them by day) during which 2508 Lancasters were lost (179 by day), representing nearly half of the

Bomber Command total. By comparison, Halifaxes flew 47,069 sorties against Germany (10,074 by day) and suffered 1467 losses.

But it would be wrong to suggest that the Lancaster prospered only because it met the narrow requirements of Sir Arthur Harris and his strategic bombing campaign. The Lancaster was a superb pilot's aircraft, and was preferred by most who sampled other bomber types. This was a crucially important attribute in an air force that was almost entirely run by pilots and former pilots, and where virtually all senior officers wore pilot's wings on their chests.

And the Lancaster's narrow focus and suitability for the pure bomber role was largely the result of its wartime genesis. The Halifax and Stirling had been designed in peacetime for the anticipated needs of war, whereas the Lancaster was designed in the light of real operational experience. Multi-role capability was not needed, whereas ease and economy of production was more important than crew comfort. Since it was clear that heavy bombers would 'live' outside, it was equally clear that the 100 ft wingspan limit that so hampered the Halifax did not have to be applied to the new Lancaster.

While attacks on area targets formed the Lancaster's 'bread and butter', what Bomber Command regarded as area attacks were often more accurate than what the USAAF thought were pinpoint 'precision attacks', especially when poor weather intervened to prevent pure visual bomb-aiming. Moreover, the Lancaster and its crews also performed some of the most daring and exciting pinpoint attack missions of the war. In the end, though, it was the bloody war of attrition waged against Germany's industrial heartland which won the conflict, and the high-profile precision attacks were relatively unimportant. In this war, the Lancaster's ability to carry a very heavy load, and to carry 'outsize' weapons, made it of critical importance.

And if the Lancaster's widespread use, popularity, superb handling characteristics and combat record were not enough to win it a place in aviation mythology, its story was one of great success dramatically grabbed from the jaws of ignominious failure – of one of the world's greatest aircraft being derived from one of the very worst.

The Lancaster entered frontline service in the early spring of 1942, and served throughout the war and even (briefly) afterwards, eventually being supplanted by the improved Lincoln (originally known as the Lancaster B IV). By 1945, Bomber Command included 56 Lancaster squadrons, and could routinely call upon around 750 frontline aircraft, with many more serving with training units and others pouring off the production lines as attrition replacements.

The scale of production and length of service ensures that the Lancaster's story is of epic proportions, and so this book concentrates on the aircraft's first two years of operational service – 1942 and 1943 – during which the seeds of victory were sown. A subsequent volume in this series will cover the Lancaster's service during 1944-45.

This 'early' period is arguably the most interesting in Bomber Command's wartime history, marking the transition from costly (and largely futile) raids by relatively small numbers of aircraft to mass raids which actually hit the Germans hard, although the alarming loss rate would remain high throughout most of the period.

ORIGINS AND DEVELOPMENT

Between the World Wars, the Air Ministry issued a succession of bomber specifications, but quite deliberately took many of them no further than the prototype stage, preferring to spend its limited budget on maximising the number of bomber aircraft in service rather than putting the new types into service. In this way, Britain kept abreast of technological and aeronautical development through the design and construction of prototypes, while keeping its bomber force at the maximum size affordable, albeit with increasingly obsolete types.

The 1930s saw priority being given to the production of twin-engined light/medium bombers, resulting in the Blenheim, Wellington and Hampden all being available in quantity when war broke out.

Long range, heavy bomber development had been virtually dormant since the introduction of the Handley Page Heyford. The Fairey Hendon, the Handley Page Harrow and Armstrong Whitworth Whitley were classified as heavy bombers, but the Hendon and Harrow carried bombloads of only 2600 lbs and 3200 lbs respectively. The Whitley, on the other hand, had a bombload of 7000 lbs, but was a development of the existing AW.23 bomber transport, with a new low-profile fuselage, and was very much an interim, expedient aircraft.

More ambitious heavy bombers resulted from two Air Ministry Specifications issued during 1936. B.12/36 called for a four-engined 'heavy', carrying a bombload of 12,000 lbs (or 24 troops when used in the transport role) and a crew of six. This Specification led to orders for two prototypes each of the Supermarine Type 317/318, and for what became the Short Stirling. Specification P.13/36 outlined a smaller aircraft, still with a six-man crew, and powered by twin Rolls-Royce Vulture engines, carrying an 8000-lb bombload or 12 troops. The Specification also included stringent performance demands, stating that the aircraft should be able to operate from existing air-fields (with standard 1500-ft grass runways) without extension. Most importantly, the Specification called for the aircraft to be capable of carrying a pair of 21-in torpe-does, and this prevented the aircraft from having the same highly com-

The elderly-looking flight engineer (left) pictured with Avro test pilot 'Bill' Thorn is chief designer Roy Chadwick, father of the Lancaster. Both men were destined to die together in the crash of the Tudor prototype on 23 August 1947 (*via Bruce Robertson*)

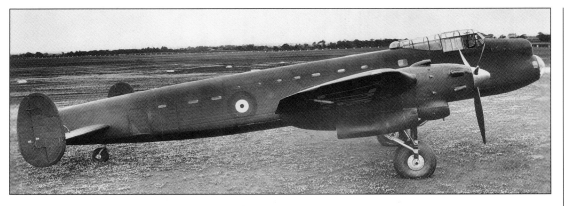

partmentalised bomb-bay as the Stirling, which could carry nothing larger than a 2000-lb bomb.

The favoured designs submitted to meet the Specification were the Handley Page HP.57 and the Avro Type 679. But while Avro pressed ahead with the Vulture-engined Type 679 to produce the Manchester, Handley Page expressed severe doubts about the Rolls-Royce engine and were ordered to redesign their bomber around four Merlin engines instead, thus producing the HP.57. The addition of two more engines required an increase in wingspan, but this was restricted by the requirement that the new aircraft be able to use existing hangars. This limited the span to 98 ft 8 in (four inches less than the maximum allowable width). Handley Page preferred radial engines, but the Air Ministry favoured the Merlin, which gave longer range but at a lower speed.

Two prototypes of the Avro Type 679 were ordered on 8 September 1936, six days after the final issue of P.13/36, and the first prototype, L7246, made its maiden flight on 25 July 1939. The Vulture engines were down on power and proved unreliable, and it was found necessary to increase the wingspan from 80 ft 2 in to 90 ft 1 in, and to add redesigned aileron hinges. The aircraft also received mass-balanced elevators and redesigned tailfins and rudders.

The Manchester suffered a host of teething troubles, with a lack of directional stability being solved by the addition of an additional central fin, and with the gun turret installations requiring refinement to cure severe airflow disturbance. Despite these problems, the Manchester was ordered in large quantities, with the aim of equipping 20 squadrons by March 1942.

Avro had been working on the four-engined Type 683 since before the prototype Manchester made its maiden flight, and the company hoped that the Ministry of Aircraft Production would eventually switch to construction of the larger bomber. In fact the decision to proceed with the four-engined bomber (the Manchester B III) was taken even before the twin-engined Manchester entered service.

The prototype Manchester looked businesslike enough, and few could have foreseen how difficult the type's birth would be. The original short-span tailplanes and very small tailfins are clearly evident (*via Francis K Mason*)

The second Manchester prototype had larger tailfins, and an auxiliary fin on the fuselage centreline. It was also fitted with nose and tail turrets (*via Bruce Robertson*)

The fourth production Manchester, L7279, was also the first to be delivered to a frontline unit, joining the newly-reformed No 207 Sqn at Waddington on 6 November 1940. One Flt Lt Sibert took the aircraft on its first raid on 23/24 February 1941, which also marked the Manchester's baptism of fire. The bomber is fitted with the early retractable 'dustbin-type' ventral gun turret. Later serving with No 61 Sqn, L7279 finished its flying career with the Royal Aircraft Establishment. It was Struck off Charge on 11 October 1943 (*via Francis K Mason*)

A No 50 Sqn Manchester sits at dispersal at Skellingthorpe in May 1942, shortly before the type's withdrawal from service. The bomber's distinctive 'high-backed' dorsal gun turret is clearly visible. Plans to produce improved Manchesters with two Centaurus or Sabre engines came to nothing, but history records that the Manchester derivative with four Merlin engines was destined for great things (*via Francis K Mason*)

When it finally reached the frontline, the Manchester proved to be severely handicapped by the unreliability of its engines, and by poor handling characteristics at high all up weights. But the aircraft was already viewed as an interim type and as a stop-gap, pending the stepping up of Halifax production, or the introduction of the Type 683.

Despite the problems with the aircraft, the Manchester equipped seven frontline squadrons within No 5 Group, and later aircraft were delivered to B IA standards with increased span tailplanes, lengthened fins and rudders designed for the Type 683, no central fin and better engine cooling. Yet despite these improvements the Manchester was a disappointment, and it suffered a heavier loss rate than any other Bomber Command type, with the exception of the Hampden.

The Manchester was always outshone by the four-engined Halifax, which proved more reliable, and more effective, and orders were cut back from more than 800 to 200 (plus the two prototypes). The Manchester flew only 1269 operations and dropped 1826 tons of bombs, while suffering a staggering 76 operational losses. Some of these fell due to the simple loss of a single engine, for unless luck was on your side, a Manchester would not normally make it home from Germany on one remaining engine, although there were exceptions.

Meanwhile, work on the four-engined Type 683 had attracted the interest of the new Ministry of Aircraft Production, although the problems affecting the Manchester prototype nearly saw the end of both Avro bomber projects. Air Marshal Sir Charles Portal, AOC-in-C Bomber Command, made the far-reaching decision that Britain's strategic bomber arm would, from the earliest possible opportunity, be

equipped solely with four-engined aircraft. At this time, the Stirling was only just entering frontline service, while the Halifax was still flying only in prototype form and the Manchester itself was five months away from entering service. Rumours of this shift in policy might have been welcomed by Avro, but on 29 July 1940 the company received a letter ordering it to cease production of the Manchester after 200 aircraft, and then switch over to licence production of the rival Halifax.

Avro immediately proposed that the Manchester should be replaced by the Type 683, an aircraft which enjoyed 70 per cent component commonality with the Manchester, and which would therefore be easy, quick and economic to manufacture. Avro were authorised to produce two prototypes of the new four-engined Manchester B III, but were expected to prepare for the possibility of manufacturing the Halifax when Manchester production ceased.

Without a formal contract (which would not be forthcoming until 15 July 1941!) Avro pressed ahead with construction of a Type 683 prototype, taking an incomplete Manchester airframe from the production line and adding an extended span wing and four Rolls-Royce Merlin Xs in Beaufighter Mk II Merlin XX type 'power-eggs'. Avro's Managing Director, Roy Dobson, directed the head of the Avro Experimental Shop, Stuart Davies, that the prototypes had to be ready and flying by 31 May 1941 (two months earlier than the Ministry of Aircraft Production had specified). Davies aimed for a first flight by 31 December 1940, and only failed to meet this because of disruption caused by a German air raid on Ringway, and by the need to change

The Manchester IA introduced a long-span tailplane with enlarged endplate fins, while the central tailfin was deleted altogether. This change made the aircraft look much more like a twin-engined Lancaster, which is hardly surprising since the Lancaster was by then in development, and both features were designed for the big four-engined bomber. This aircraft, L7515, is seen here whilst serving with No 207 Sqn. A long-lived machine, it subsequently spent time with Nos 106 and 49 Sqns, followed by a spell with No 1656 Conversion Unit. L7571 was Struck off Charge on 6 November 1943 (*via Francis K Mason*)

First prototype Lancaster (BT308) is seen at a misty Boscombe Down in late January 1941. The aircraft has a Manchester-type tail unit and small Manchester mainwheels, while the early shroud around the rear turret is also visible. This was designed to prevent airflow disturbing the elevators when the turret was rotated. It proved unnecessary and was dropped (*via Bruce Robertson*)

large parts of the hydraulic system to avoid the problems then afflicting the basic Manchester.

Poor weather in early January then delayed the first flight until 9 January 1941. The aircraft, carrying the serial number BT308, was officially known as the Manchester III, although the clearance to fly certificate used the new Lancaster name, which was officially approved on 27 January.

BT308 was duly sent to the Aeroplane and Armament Experimental Establishment (A&AEE) at Boscombe Down on 27 January, and a handling report was issued on 3 March 1941. By this time the aircraft was back with Avro, undergoing modifications.

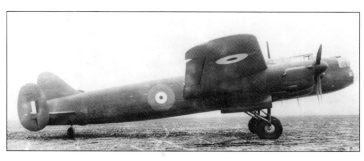

The first prototype had originally boasted the Manchester-style triple-finned short-span tail unit, but within six weeks had received the enlarged twin-fins and extended span tailplanes associated with the Manchester B IA. The aircraft was also re-engined with Merlin XX engines, and these were used for speed trials at Boscombe Down. The latter were something of a revelation, since the aircraft proved to be about ten per cent faster than Avro's estimates. This was because the close-cowled engine installation produced much lower drag than the Merlin installation in Bomber Command's ancient-looking Whitleys.

The second Lancaster prototype, DG595, made its maiden flight on 13 May 1941, but delivery to the A&AEE at Boscombe Down was delayed while the Establishment worked through a backlog of trials and evaluation work. Chief Designer Roy Chadwick then used the time to further refine and improve the aircraft.

Avro received a contract for its two prototypes (and for two further prototypes, to be fitted with Bristol Hercules radial engines, as an insurance policy) on 15 July 1941. The first of these aircraft, DT810, made its maiden flight on 26 November 1941, but the second was cancelled. At much the same time that the contract was issued, the company received orders for 100 aircraft that had originally been contracted as Manchesters to be completed as Lancasters – 43 by Avro and 57 by Metropolitan Vickers. On 6 June 1941 the order was increased to 454.

Service trials at Boscombe Down were generally successful, but showed the need for improved wingtips. The outer wing panels were extended, bringing the total span to 102 ft, and increasing the number of wing fuel tanks from four to six. A handful of early production aircraft (the first of which, L7527, had flown on 31 October) had to be retrofitted with the new outer wing panels. The first production aircraft was the first Lancaster flown in the dark green, dark earth and black colour scheme which came to characterise the type, and looked more warlike than the 'yellow-bellied' prototypes. But close examination

Before and after photographs of BT308's tail modifications. Also evident are the unusual Beaufighter-type engine cowlings, with their single external stub pipe. Both photos were taken at Ringway about three weeks apart. This machine subsequently spent time with Nos 44, 97 and 207 Sqns between September 1941 and January 1942 as these units familiarised themselves with the new heavy bomber. Passed on to Rolls-Royce in February 1942, BT308 was then assigned to the Directorate of Technical Development and loaned to Armstrong Whitworth, who installed the experimental Metrovick F2/1 turbojet engine in its rear fuselage. Sadly, this historically significant aircraft was Struck off Charge on 30 May 1944 and duly scrapped (*via Francis K Mason*)

would have revealed that the 'guns' installed in the tail turret were no more than painted broomsticks.

Trials of early production aircraft at Boscombe Down resulted in a release to service on Christmas Eve 1941. On the same day, No 44 Sqn at Waddington received its first three Lancasters, although the first prototype had visited the station in mid-September for familiarisation, and to ensure that aircraft and airfield were fully compatible.

No 44 Sqn was previously equipped with the Handley Page Hampden. Other Hampden units were re-equipped with the Manchester between October 1941 and April 1942, although this was hardly much of an improvement. The Hampden was under-armed, and the cramped fuselage made the type uncomfortable on long range missions, but the bomber was fast and surprisingly agile, and the Manchester offered little other than increased payload/range capability and (theoretically) an even better maximum speed. This was weighed against a much worse loss rate, which saw the average Manchester clocking up only 16.7 sorties before being lost, while the average Hampden completed 27.25 operations.

Fortunately, most of the ex-Hampden squadrons kept the appalling Manchesters for only a matter of months before ditching them in favour of Lancasters. And whereas redundant Bomber Command Hampdens found a new operational role with Coastal Command (and some were even exported to a grateful Russia), the Manchesters were briefly relegated to second-line duties and then scrapped. But while replacing Hampdens with Manchesters may have been stupidity, replacing either type with the Lancaster represented a real leap forward.

Apart from its bright yellow undersides and circled P-prototype markings, the second Lancaster prototype, DG595, looked very similar to the production aircraft which followed. The early, unfaired mid-upper gun turret is noteworthy. Utilised by Avro to further develop the design's offensive capabilities, DG595 undertook ballistic trials with the Royal Aircraft Establishment in March 1943, before being passed on to the Torpedo Development Unit later in the year. It was Struck off Charge on 17 February 1944 (*via Francis K Mason*)

L7527 was the first production Lancaster (first flight on 31 October 1941), and it is seen here before the application of black undersides and the installation of a mid-upper turret. Retained by Avro until November 1942, the bomber was then assigned to No 1654 Heavy Conversion Unit. Passed on to No XV Sqn in early March 1944, L7527 was lost on the 27th of that same month during a raid on Essen (*via Bruce Robertson*)

1942 – SURVIVAL

The Lancaster arrived with Bomber Command at a difficult time for the organisation. A survey of individual aircraft bombing photographs (contained within the Butt report) revealed that even the best crews (whose aircraft tended to be the only ones equipped with cameras at that stage of the war) were achieving very much lower accuracy figures than had been assumed. Overall, only one in four crews claiming to have bombed a target (theirs were the photos surveyed) had got within five miles of it, while in cloudy conditions the figure dropped to one in fifteen! Even on clear summer nights, fewer than half of the crews dropped their bombs within five miles of their target. Figures for targets in Germany were slightly worse.

Following the report, AOC-in-C Bomber Command, Air Marshal Sir Richard Peirse (who had replaced Sir Charles Portal in October 1940 when the latter had become Chief of the Air Staff) switched the focus of his offensive to easier, lower priority targets, less well protected by flak, searchlights, fighters and the Ruhr's natural defence of mist and haze. But even against these targets, it was clear that crews were becoming less willing to press home their attacks, and many suspected that the Command was beginning to suffer a crisis of confidence.

Nor were these modest results being obtained cheaply. During a four-month period from 7/8 July to 10 November 1941, Bomber Command had lost 526 aircraft – equivalent to its entire frontline strength! Aircraft were relatively easy to replace, but the losses of trained crews presented a much more difficult problem. Air Marshal Peirse was ordered to scale down operations while the future of the Bomber Offensive was examined and debated.

Peirse himself had done his best with the limited and inadequate resources at his disposal, presiding over a Command with obsolete or unsuitable aircraft, and with insufficient navigation equipment to achieve the degree of bombing accuracy required. Yet by attempting to fulfil its task, the Command had suffered heavy losses, losing many of its most senior and highly skilled aircrew who had trained before the war. But although he had been provided with 'shoddy tools', Peirse himself was destined to shoulder the blame for the Command's failure.

He was removed from his post on 8 January 1942, and was temporarily replaced by the AOC

No 44 Sqn at Waddington received its first Lancasters on Christmas Eve 1941, trading in its twin-engined Hampdens. The units CO was Wg Cdr Roderick Alastair Brook Learoyd, who had won a VC for a daring low level attack on the Dortmund Ems canal in a Blenheim in August 1940. Although wearing No 44 Sqn's KM codes, L7578 was only briefly used by the unit, being assigned instead to No 97 Sqn. Subsequently passed on to No 83 Sqn, the aircraft spent time with Nos 1654 and 1668 HCUs, before being written off in a crash at Gonalston on 26 May 1944 whilst serving with No 5 Lancaster Finishing School (*via Francis K Mason*)

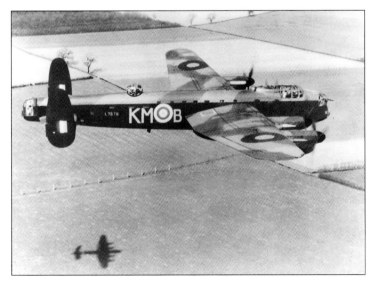

No 3 Group, Air Vice Marshal J E A Baldwin, while the War Cabinet, the Air Ministry and others formulated a new strategy for Bomber Command, and searched for someone to spearhead it. Early in the war, Bomber Command had been forced to abandon day bombing and seek the sanctuary of night, which had now itself been shown insufficient to protect the bombers, or to allow them to hit their targets. The very future of the strategic bombing offensive lay in the balance.

The idea that strategic bombing alone would bring Germany to its knees, causing a domestic collapse and reducing the need for an invasion and prolonged land campaign, was largely discredited. Few still believed that the pinpoint bombing of individual factories and economic targets would ever 'destroy the foundations of the German war machine', or the morale of the German people.

In the end, the decision to continue the strategic bombing campaign was made largely on pragmatic and political grounds. With Britain's new Russian ally fighting for its life in the east, Bomber Command was the only means by which the RAF could take the fight to the enemy, and was thus the only means by which Churchill could 'hold up his head' in dealings with Stalin.

The bomber enthusiasts exploited the fact that Bomber Command was supposedly the only arm of Britain's armed forces hitting the Germans in the west (conveniently forgetting the army in the Western Desert, and the joint forces battling in the Atlantic) and drew up a plan for a revolutionary new bomber offensive. This entailed a programme of 'continuous attack' against 43 leading German industrial cities, with their combined population of 15 million. Such attacks would be against the cities themselves, and not just against factories within them, and it was calculated that a bomber force of 4000 aircraft would produce complete collapse within six months. Churchill rejected the plan, but threw his weight behind Bomber Command's continuation of a Strategic Offensive at its existing strength, and tacitly approved

The very sharp-eyed might notice a solitary Manchester (third from the left, serial R5780/OL-D) in this evocative view of No 83 Sqn setting out on a raid to Bremen from Scampton on 25 June 1942. This was to be the Manchester's last fling, with four units despatching 18 aircraft on the mission (*via Bruce Robertson*)

A few hours after this shot was taken on 25 June 1942, again at Scampton, Lancaster B I R5620/OL-H was shot down over Bremen. The aircraft's captain on this mission was Plt Off J R Farrow. At this stage of the war, Bomber Command's operations were costly and achieved relatively little material affect, and the young crews were statistically unlikely to survive a full tour of operations (*via Francis K Mason*)

the switch from an attempt at precision bombing to a deliberate area bombing strategy.

On 14 February 1942, Bomber Command received a directive (drafted by Air Vice Marshal Bottomley) confirming the change of emphasis. This stated that 'The Primary Objective of your operation should now be focused on the morale of the enemy civil population, and in particular of the industrial workers'. In a subsequent letter to Bottomley, Portal, Chief of the Air Staff wanted it made clear that henceforth 'aiming points are to be built up areas, and not, for instance, the dockyards or aircraft factories'. The new policy was formulated by the War Cabinet and the Air Ministry, and Bomber Command had little input into it. Nor did the Command's new AOC-in-C – Air Chief Marshal Sir Arthur Harris – appointed eight days later, although his fierce approval and championing of the policy made many think that it was his own.

Harris inherited a Command which his predecessors had ensured would soon be in good shape, even if he would never get the 4000-strong fleet of aircraft which many had demanded. The hopeless Manchester, the ageing Hampden and the prehistoric Whitley would all be gone by the end of 1942, replaced by Halifaxes, Stirlings and Lancasters. Aircraft were also being equipped with the *Gee* navigation system, which allowed bombers to find closer targets, including Bremen, Emden, the Rhineland, the Ruhr and Wilhelmshaven, and which was a powerful aid in helping lost bombers recover to Britain.

Harris did bring some originality to Bomber Command, however, most notably in his enthusiasm for incendiaries and his single-minded attention to concentrating raids into the shortest possible time-frame in order to overwhelm the defences and emergency services. Harris aimed to use blast bombs to blow off roofs and blow out windows, to block roads with rubble, and to hinder the fire brigades, while dropping huge numbers of incendiaries which would take hold in the roofless, windowless buildings. 'It's easier to burn a city down than it is to blow it up', he once famously remarked.

The use of blast bombs was valuable even when fires did not take hold, for there was always the temptation to repair buildings whose windows had merely been blown out, at great cost in resources and man-power, diverting them from other areas of the economy, and usually only for a temporary period before the bombers struck again.

Although Harris has gained a reputation as having been some-

The RAF had five underground bomb storage depots. Ordnance did not remain in store for long, since the arrival of the Lancaster and Halifax led to an enormous consumption rate – although few were destined to do much more than frighten farm animals in the general vicinity of target cities in 1942! (*via Bruce Robertson*)

At the bomber airfields bombs were usually stored in the open in reveted, often wooded or heavily camouflaged dumps, placed a safe distance away from aircraft and other base infrastructure (*via Bruce Robertson*)

Armourers load four 250-lb bombs into the cavernous bomb-bay of a Lancaster, fitting them in front of a 4000-lb 'Cookie'. The Lancaster's huge, unobstructed bomb-bay allowed it to carry the widest possible range of weapons, making it more useful than aircraft such as the Stirling, whose bomb-bay was highly compartmentalised (*Aerospace Publishing*)

Homing pigeons were a little-known addition to the bomber crew, and sometimes proved useful, especially when aircraft were forced to ditch. Pigeons could be released in flight, although the aircraft's slipstream made this hazardous, and they were unable to fly in cloud (*Aerospace Publishing*)

thing of an impatient, fire-breathing, hard-driving martinet, who pushed the strategic bomber offensive forward with extraordinary energy, he was in fact a master strategist. And although he presided over bursts of frenetic activity, he was happy to hold back his forces when weather conditions, or the state of the moon, promised little chance of success. Remarkably, Harris's first three months at the helm saw a lower level of activity, and lower bomb tonnages than the same period the previous year.

When he took over the reins at Bomber Command's High Wycombe headquarters, Harris (known to the press and public as 'Bomber' Harris, or 'Butch' to his intimates) had two Lancaster units in the process of forming. No 44 Sqn had received its first aircraft on Christmas Eve 1941, while No 97 Sqn followed in January 1942. The Lancaster had almost flown its first operation (a mining mission of Aas Fjord, aimed at bottling up the German battleship *Tirpitz*) on 25 January, but had been prevented from doing so by the unserviceability of the planned forward operating base at Wick.

No 97 Sqn was loaned the first prototype, BT308, on 10 January to begin conversion, and soon began to receive production aircraft.

Lancaster operations finally began on 3/4 March, when No 44 Sqn despatched four aircraft to 'garden' (mine) 'Yams' and 'Rosemary' (the approach to Heligoland, and an area further north) each with four 'vegetables' (mines). A week later, on 10/11 March, No 44 Sqn contributed two aircraft to a raid on Essen, and sent another against Köln three nights later. No 97 Sqn began Lancaster operations on 20 March, despatching six aircraft on a 'gardening' mission at 'Willows' (Swinemünde, in the Baltic). Poor weather caused three aircraft to divert to bases in Oxfordshire on their return.

The first operational Lancaster loss occurred on 24/25 March, when No 44 Sqn's Flt Sgt Warren-Smith failed to return from a mining sortie. The largest-scale Lancaster mission to date occurred on 25/26 March when seven Lancasters drawn from both squadrons, and equipped with *Gee*, were sent out as part of a 254-aircraft raid on Essen. Although 181 crews claimed to have bombed the city, many were drawn off by a well-constructed decoy, and German records showed that only nine bombs and 700 incendiaries fell on the town, destroying one house, damaging two more and killing five people. Bomber Command lost nine aircraft in achieving this modest success.

By the end of March the Command had received 54 Lancasters, ten of them going to a third unit, No 207 Sqn, forming that same month. Nos 44 and 97 Sqns spent much of March preparing for the Augsburg raid in mid-April, and this is described in detail in Chapter Three.

There was thus no Lancaster participation in the successful raid on Lübeck on 28/29 March, which caused £20 million worth of damage, killed 320 people and destroyed the Drägerwerke factory, which was of critical importance in U-boat construction – 12 of the 234 aircraft sortied failed to return. Nor was the Lancaster involved in Bomber Command's next major operation, a 263-aircraft raid against Köln.

Seven Lancasters participated in the raid on Hamburg on 8/9 April, however, but only about a dozen of the aircraft despatched (272 in total) dropped their bombs on the city. Eight Lancasters were despatched against Essen on 10/11 April, although the ordnance dropped by the 172 aircraft that claimed to bomb (of 254 sortied) was widely scattered, and only about six aircraft hit the city.

A week after the Augsburg raid a single Lancaster from No 97 Sqn participated in a 161-aircraft attack against Rostock on 23/24 April, which enjoyed only limited success. A similar raid the next night (including two No 97 and three No 207 Sqn Lancasters) was little more successful, and a follow-up on 25/26 (with each unit despatching four Lancasters) at last set major portions of the city alight, while the Manchesters of No 106 Sqn, led by Guy Gibson, hit the Heinkel factory for the first time. A final raid against Rostock on 26/27 April did even more damage, prompting Goebbels to coin the phrase *Terrorangriff* (terror raid) for the first time. It involved a single No 97 Sqn Lancaster. Nos 44 and 97 Sqns were involved in raids against the *Tirpitz* on 27 April, and these are described in detail in Chapter Four.

No 61 Sqn converted to the Lancaster during April 1942, while No 207 Sqn continued to work up to full operational status. The unit's conversion took only 24 days from delivery of the first Lancaster to being declared operational on the new type. No 207 Sqn was the first to see a new crew concept, with the traditional 'second pilot' being replaced by a dedicated flight engineer. Eleven former second pilots were given 'captaincies' very quickly (perhaps too quickly), and five of these would be killed within six weeks. No 83 Sqn received its first Lancasters in late April, and worked up during May 1942.

One No 207 Sqn machine that just escaped becoming a casualty was the Lancaster flown by Sqn Ldr Kenneth Beauchamp, which was conducting a mining sortie on the night of 22/23 May. After losing one engine, Beauchamp was momentarily blinded by searchlights as he crossed the enemy coast, and he hit the sea, buckling both starboard propellers. Despite having to shut down the starboard inner, Beauchamp nursed the aircraft up to 1000 ft, and limped back to base on two engines.

Following the success of the series of raids against Rostock, Bomber Command sent out a succession of attacks against Stuttgart in early May. The first raid was a failure, with bombs being widely scattered due to poor weather, thick cloud cover and a realistic decoy site at the nearby town of Lauffen. The second attack was no more successful, and nor was the third, flown on 6/7 May. Two No 207 Sqn Lancasters were attacked by fighters and Wt Off Stott's tail gunner actually shot one Bf 109 down. Wt Off Lamb's aircraft had one engine put out of action and it crashed on approach, although the crew escaped injury.

A mission against Warnemünde on 8/9 May proved even more costly. The 193 aircraft despatched included 21 Lancasters, and four of these, all from No 44 Sqn, and including its new CO, Wg Cdr Lynch-Bloss, failed to return. Bomber Command hit Mannheim on 19/20 May, despatching 197 aircraft, including 13 Lancasters. Only a handful of bombs hit the city, however, and German casualties amounted to two firemen. All the Lancasters returned to base, but 11 aircraft did not.

This mission was typical of Bomber Command's poor 'rate of return' during early 1942, and showed how little had changed under Harris. The next major Lancaster mission was a raid on the Gnome Le

The Lancaster's tail turret looked formidable, with its four 0.303-in machine guns. But cannon armed enemy fighters could stand off outside range, while manoeuvring the heavy turret could present problems in the event of hydraulic failure, and it was difficult for gunners to maintain concentration in the often bitter and intense cold (*Aerospace Publishing*)

Entry to the rear turret was via this relatively narrow hatch, exposed as these armourers fit the 0.303-in Brownings. To escape, the rear gunner had to rotate the turret and scramble out backwards, encumbered by his bulky sheepskin Irvine jacket, trousers and parachute (*via Bruce Robertson*)

The guns of a No 57 Sqn B I receive pre-flight care and attention. This photograph shows to advantage the fairing installed to improve airflow around the base of the turret, and to physically prevent the gunner from hitting parts of the airframe when he fired his guns! W4190 served exclusively with No 57 Sqn in the frontline, before being transferred to No 1660 HCU in February 1943. It was written off when it crashed on take-off from Winthorpe on 23 August 1943 (*via Bruce Robertson*)

Rhône engine factory at Paris Gennevilliers, with the 77-aircraft force including 14 Lancasters, three of them drawn from the newly-formed No 83 Sqn. Five aircraft were lost, but all of the Lancasters returned to base safely, although the factory escaped significant damage.

The success of the raids on Lübeck and Rostock provided a great boost for Harris, but for every success there were several failures, and Bomber Command's future remained under threat. What was needed was a morale-boosting spectacular, which Harris provided in the form of the first Thousand Bomber raid.

This was an incredible achievement, not least because Harris could call on only about 400 frontline aircraft and trained crews from Bomber Command's frontline units, forcing him to boost numbers by using aircraft and crews from his operational training units. The latter units did not only send instructor aircrew – of the 208 aircraft provided by No 91 Group, for example, 49 took off captained by student pilots. Harris had originally planned on using up to 250 bombers from Coastal Command and a handful from Flying Training Command.

The latter organisation initially offered 50 Wellingtons, but most of these were inadequately equipped for night bombing, and in the end the Command provided only four Vickers bombers for the first Thousand Bomber Raid. The Admiralty, unwilling to participate in what it saw as a PR exercise, forbade Coastal Command participation altogether, fearful of losing control of its handful of long range aircraft. But despite these setbacks, Harris managed to launch 1047 aircraft on his first Raid, against Köln, on 30 May 1942. The magnificent cathedral city of Köln was actually Harris's second choice, but poor weather three nights running ruled out his preferred target of Hamburg.

Köln's relative proximity to Bomber Command's East Anglian bases, and its position on the river Rhine (highly visible to H_2S, and within *Gee* range), made it a common 'fall-back' target when weather or heavy losses ruled out hitting more distant cities. Quite apart from the Thousand Bomber Raid, Köln was hit again and again, and 10,000 unexploded high explosive bombs were found in the city after the war had ended. The

thousands of unexploded incendiaries were not counted, nor was the total of exploded bombs or unexploded bombs found during the war ever tallied up.

The mission included 73 Lancasters, all drawn from No 5 Group. All 15 aircraft from the recently-formed No 83 Sqn sortied, as did 11 from the even newer No 106 Sqn. This unit had never previously flown a Lancaster 'op', although all its crews were 'old hands' on the Manchester. One aircraft was also sent out by No 50 Sqn, although this unit's crews had

After mid-1942, the Lancaster's spacious and well-lit cockpit accommodated the pilot (to port) and flight engineer to starboard. Before then, most squadrons had carried a second pilot in the right-hand seat (*Aerospace Publishing*)

gained little experience on the Manchester, and were still more familiar with the more nimble Hampden, and had therefore taken longer to convert onto the Lancaster.

No 4 Group provided 131 Halifaxes, while No 3 Group's contribution included 88 Stirlings. But the backbone of the raid was provided by 602 Wellingtons, 299 of them from Bomber Command's frontline groups, and the rest from operational training units and Flying Training Command. According to Bomber Command records, 868 aircraft attacked the primary target, dropping 1455 tons of bombs (mainly incendiaries) and destroying 3330 buildings and damaging many others. The raid killed between 469 and 486 Germans, most of them civilians, and injured 5027 more. Some 45,132 people were 'bombed out' of their homes, and an estimated 150,000 fled the city.

A single Lancaster was shot down, together with 40 other RAF bombers, and it was calculated that casualty rates reduced as the German defences were progressively overwhelmed. The OTU crews thus suffered a lower loss rate than the frontline groups, and the aircraft captained by student pilots suffered less than those skippered by instructors. Churchill had been prepared for the loss of up to 100 aircraft, and thus saw the raid as a great success, and as a signal demonstration of Bomber Command's importance and significance.

The wireless operator's station was cramped and claustrophobic, being located on the port side aft of the navigator (seen in the background here), who sat facing to port behind the pilot's seat
(*via Bruce Robertson*)

In addition to the bombers, 49 No 2 Group Blenheims, plus 39 from Fighter Command and 15 from Army Co-operation Command were despatched on intruder missions against German nightfighter aerodromes along the route to be followed by the bomber stream to Köln.

While the press and public seized upon the sheer number of aircraft involved in these 'spectaculars', the tactics used were even more

All of the crew's efforts (and those of the army of riggers, fitters, armourers and other ground trades) were focused on ensuring that the bomb-aimer pressed this innocuous little button at exactly the right moment, which meant that the Lancaster's deadly bombload fell on its intended target. That, at least, was the theory, although in 1942 accuracy was woefully poor (*via Bruce Robertson*)

Women workers put the finishing touches to a Merlin at Rolls-Royce's Derby factory. The Merlin proved to be the ideal powerplant for the Lancaster in British Rolls-Royce- or US Packard-built forms. Ironically, the Halifax proved more successful when re-engined with the Hercules radial (*via Bruce Robertson*)

significant. During the war's early raids, 100 aircraft had taken up to four hours to attack a typical target, while the two-hour attack by 234 aircraft at Lubeck was regarded as being revolutionary. But the 'Bomber Stream' used in the Thousand Bomber Raids funnelled all participating aircraft through the target in an astonishing 90 minutes.

This ensured that the aircraft passed through the minimum number of German nightfighter boxes, reducing the chances of interception, and also ensured that flak and searchlight defences at the target would also be overwhelmed. German airspace was divided into a network of boxes, each controlled by a single Ground Controlled Intercept (GCI) controller. He could only direct a maximum of six intercepts per hour, meaning that if 1000 aircraft passed through his 'box' in one hour, only six would be intercepted.

Passing the maximum number of aircraft over the target in the minimum time-scale also ensured that fire brigades on the ground would be overwhelmed by the quantity of incendiaries being dropped. Harris had originally planned to launch a couple of Thousand Bomber Raids during every suitable moon period. In the event, there would only be three of these 'maximum effort' attacks, and after these subsequent raids, they would never again rely so heavily on aircraft from the OTUs and training units.

Harris kept his Köln strike force together for a follow-up attack on Essen two nights later on 1/2 June 1942. Although billed as another Thousand Bomber Raid, only 956 aircraft could be assembled, and 74 of these were Lancasters – 31 bombers failed to return, including four Lancasters. Haze or thin cloud cover made it difficult to find the target, and most bombers failed to bomb Essen, which suffered the loss of 11 houses, 15 civilian dead and a burned-out PoW working camp. Oberhausen, Duisburg and Mülheim suffered rather worse, with a total of 150 deaths, and bombs fell on some 11 Ruhr towns.

Essen was re-visited by 195 aircraft (including 27 Lancasters) on 2/3 June with even less success, and with the loss of 14 more bombers, including two Lancasters. The town was attacked again on 5/6 June, 8/9 June and 16/17 June, each time without much effect. Over the course of the three attacks, some 61 civilians were killed for the loss of 39 bombers, including four Lancasters. Bremen was attacked by 170 aircraft on 3/4 June, losing 83 of its populace and several streets of housing, although the U-boat yards and Focke-Wulf factories in the town escaped serious damage.

Emden also came under attack at this time, with raids on 6/7, 19/20, 20/21 and 22/23 June that saw a total of 32 aircraft, including two Lancasters, lost. Emden's residential areas were hit quite hard, and 23 residents were killed, although two of the raids were drawn off by decoy fires or inaccurate marking by the 'flare force', and on these nights no Germans lost their lives at all – while Bomber Command lost 17 bombers with their crews.

Bremen was the target of the third and final Thousand Force raid. Bomber Command sent out 960 aircraft (including the normally diurnal Bostons and Mosquitos of No 2 Group). Lancasters accounted for ten per cent of the Bomber Command force, with 96 aircraft sortied.

These included 16 Lancasters each from Nos 83, 97 and 207 Sqns, 17 from No 106, 14 from No 61 and 12 from No 44 Sqn.

The Bomber Command aircraft were augmented by 102 Coastal Command Hudsons and Wellingtons and five Army Co-operation Command Blenheims. These assets took the total to 1067 aircraft, which transited through the target area in only 65 minutes. Bremen was within *Gee* range, so the leading aircraft were able to bomb despite cloud cover, achieving a degree of accuracy. A strengthening wind 'fanned the flames' and helped the destruction, totalling 572 houses (with 6108 more damaged) and 85 Bremeners killed. Most of the force 'area bombed' the city, but No 5 Group was tasked with attacking the Focke-Wulf factory (which suffered significant damage) and Coastal Command hit the Deschimag shipyard.

The scale of the damage should not be over-stated, for the Germans were convinced that only 80 RAF aircraft had bombed the town, and claimed that 52 of these had been shot down. Subsequent BBC broadcasts claiming that 'a thousand bombers' had been despatched were taken as propaganda aimed at making the losses more palatable to the British public! German claims were fairly close to the mark, with 44 aircraft shot down in the target area and four more falling on their way back across the North Sea. In absolute terms, this was Bomber Command's heaviest loss of the war so far, although in percentile terms the loss was relatively light, at five per cent.

Bremen was attacked again on 27/28 June by 144 aircraft, including 24 Lancasters, on 29/30 June by 253 aircraft, including 64 Lancasters, and on 2/3 July by 325 aircraft, including 53 Lancasters. Bomber Command losses on all three nights totalled 33 aircraft, including two Lancasters. Civilian casualties were exceptionally light in a city which had become used to air raids, but damage was considerable, and the Focke-Wulf factory and U-boat yards were further damaged. The second raid, on 29/30 June, marked the first occasion on which four-engined bombers accounted for more than half of the aircraft sent out on a major large-scale raid, with 145 of the 253 aircraft being 'heavies'.

Although Lancaster losses were negligible, the number of aircraft offered by the various squadrons diminished appreciably with each new raid due to unserviceability. No 106 Sqn sent out 17 aircraft on

A Bristol Hercules radial engine on the wing of a Lancaster B II. The Hercules-powered variant had been designed in anticipation of the supply of Merlin engines being disrupted by America's entry into the war. Some expected that US industry would cease production of this 'foreign' engine in favour of indigenous powerplants, and that the pressure on Merlin production would then become unbearable. In fact, the USA would dramatically increase Merlin production, making US-built Merlin engines available to a range of British-built aircraft types, as well as powering the bulk of the P-51 Mustangs constructed for both the USAAF and the RAF (*via Bruce Robertson*)

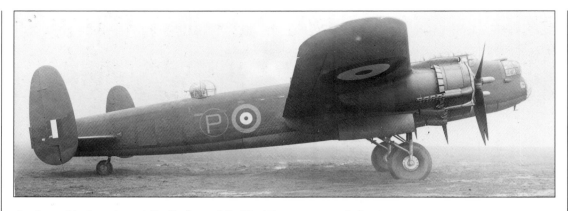

the first raid, then six and finally five, while No 97 was more typical, sending 16, then 11 and then nine. No 207 Sqn (whose groundcrew were used to the recalcitrant Manchester) ensured that the unit was the exception to the general rule, offering 16 aircraft for the first two raids and 14 for the last. Their hard work was noticed, and No 207 Sqn's most senior groundcrew were rapidly posted to the other units to pass on their experience and knowledge.

Scampton-based No 49 Sqn converted to the Lancaster during June 1942, and within five months the unit would be sufficiently regarded to be selected to lead the mass raid on Le Creusot, as described in Chapter Three.

The next major raid was against Wilhelmshaven on 8/9 July, involving 285 aircraft, 52 of which were Lancasters. Few bombs hit the town, and those that did destroyed a dockyard restaurant, a department store, the harbourmaster's office and a bus garage with 30 buses inside! Twenty-five of Wilhelmshaven's population were killed and five bombers failed to return.

After the raid against Danzig on 11 July (described in Chapter Three), the Lancasters next major raid was against Duisburg on 13/14 July. This was a continuation of Bomber Command's run of bad luck, achieving little and with ten aircraft failing to return from a mission that killed 17 German civilians. The 194 aircraft despatched included 13 Lancasters, one of which was lost.

Things went better on 19/20 July, when 99 four-engined bombers attacked the Vulkan U-boat works at Vegesack. The target was covered by cloud and the force bombed using *Gee*, and although all bombs missed their target, they did completely destroy two storehouses full of

The easy availability of the Packard Merlin made the Lancaster B II almost irrelevant before it had entered service, but 1000 were ordered from Armstrong Whitworth in 1941 (and 300 built). The Bristol Hercules-engined Lancaster climbed rather faster than the Merlin-powered aircraft up to about 18,000 ft, and was about as fast in the cruise and 'flat out'. Unfortunately, the aircraft had a lower operational ceiling. The prototype, DT810, seen here, made its maiden flight on 26 November 1941. Following testing with the A&AEE, RAE and Bristol, the bomber was assigned to the Directorate of Technical Development and finally Struck off Charge in 1944 (*Aerospace Publishing*)

The third Lancaster unit to form was No 207 Sqn, formerly equipped with Manchesters, which converted at Bottesford, in Leicestershire, from March 1942. One of the unit's early B Is is seen here during a training exercise (*via Bruce Robertson*)

L7580 of No 207 Sqn was displayed in Trafalgar Square during a 'Wings for Victory' fund-raising event in 1942. The aircraft returned to No 207 Sqn as EM-C and was withdrawn from ops in late 1943, subsequently serving with a succession of training units and surviving until Struck off Charge in November 1945 (*via Bruce Robertson*)

military equipment (valued at £100,000) in nearby Bremen, and burned down a wooden-hutted military camp. None of the 28 Lancasters were lost, although three of 40 Halifaxes failed to return.

Duisburg was the target for the next series of raids, on 21/22, 23/24 and 25/26 July. These involved 291, 215 and 313 aircraft respectively, including 29, 45 and 33 Lancasters. These attacks cost Bomber Command 31 aircraft and killed 120 Germans, but destroyed a number of houses. Casualties were heavier than normal on the first attack, which was despatched on a moonless night in an attempt to frustrate the nightfighters. Most losses occurred in the coastal fighter belt.

Hamburg was attacked on 26/27 and 28/29 July by heavy forces of 403 and 256 bombers respectively. The first night's attack included 77 Lancasters, two of which were among the 29 aircraft which failed to return. The first night resulted in the destruction of 823 houses and £25 million worth of damage, killing 337 people. Another 14,000 were bombed out. The second attack involved only No 3 Group and the OTUs, since poor weather grounded Nos 1, 4 and 5 Groups. Poor weather forced most of the OTU machines to turn back, and 68 aircraft bombed in the target area. Some 31 bombers failed to return.

The next night Bomber Command switched its attention to Saarbrücken, causing heavy damage. Nine of the 291 aircraft despatched – including two Lancasters – failed to return. An even bigger effort was launched against Düsseldorf on 31 July/1 August, and this raid marked the first time that more than 100 Lancasters were sent out against a single target. Two Avro bombers were amongst the 29 aircraft which failed to return. Düsseldorf and nearby Neuss had

279 of their inhabitants killed and 12,053 bombed out, and damage was heavy.

Duisburg was again the target on 6/7 August, when 216 aircraft were despatched. Accuracy was poor and five aircraft were lost. Some 192 bombers were sent out against Osnabrück on 9/10 August, including 42 Lancasters. Damage was heavy, and only six attacking aircraft failed to return.

An anonymous Lancaster awaits its deadly load of incendiaries sometime during 1942. Few early Lancasters survived long, and when a bomber was shot down, its crew had a statistically poorer chance of survival than their comrades in the rival Halifax (*via Bruce Robertson*)

Mainz suffered two heavy attacks on 11/12 and 12/13 August by 154 and 138 aircraft respectively. These caused substantial damage and heavy casualties, and cost only 11 aircraft.

Bomber Command's last major attack before the formation of the Pathfinder Force on 17 August was a 131-aircraft attack on Düsseldorf, which caused little damage and only one fatal casualty, although four bombers were lost.

It should perhaps be pointed out that the Bomber Command casualty rate had by now reached 4.3 per cent, meaning that the average bomber aircrew had only an 11 per cent chance of surviving a full tour of duty. At that time, bomber crews were expected to complete an initial tour of 30 ops, with a further 20-op second tour following a 'rest'. Before Harris took over, the loss rate had been as low as 2.5 per cent, giving the same crew a 28.2 per cent chance of surviving 50 trips.

But while a loss rate of four per cent or above was unacceptable to individual crew-members, it was unsustainable for the force as a whole, threatening to leave insufficient experienced crews to provide the necessary continuity and leadership. This process had been starkly demonstrated in the Halifax squadrons of No 4 Group, which suffered a 6.2 per cent casualty rate between March and August 1942, resulting in a one month rest from operations.

On the same day (17 August) that the Pathfinders formed, the USAAF's Eighth Air Force mounted its first mission. From then on, the Allies moved inexorably towards a round-the-clock bombing offensive against the Third Reich. That night also witnessed the last Bomber Command operation by the Bristol Blenheim. But the first major raid of what should have been a new era was disappointing, with five aircraft failing to return from a raid against Osnabrück which failed to cause much damage, and which killed only seven of the town's citizens. The first raid actually directed by the Pathfinders was even less successful. Strong winds caused the 31 marker aircraft to miss the town of Flensburg, and the 87 Main Force bombers mainly attacked two Danish towns, fortunately without causing heavy casualties.

The second Pathfinder-led attack was no more successful, and although 226 aircraft were despatched against Frankfurt on 24/25 August, damage was light, and 16 bombers failed to return, six of them Lancasters. The Pathfinder force finally demonstrated what it could do at Kassel on 27/28 August, illuminating the target for a devastating Main Force raid, although 31 of the 306 aircraft despatched were lost.

On 28/29 August the Pathfinders marked Nuremberg using the newly developed Target Indicators, and the 159 aircraft despatched caused considerable damage, especially to the wooden *Kraft durch Freude* ('Strength through Joy') town south of the city, which burned down. No 106 Sqn (fresh from the attack on Gdynia the day before) dropped two 8000-lb blast bombs, adding to the devastation. Casualties, though, were heavy, with 23 aircraft lost, including four of 71 Lancasters. The overall loss rate was an unsustainable 14.5 per cent, while 34 per cent of the Wellingtons failed to return.

The month of August also saw the conversion of No IX Sqn onto the Lancaster. Following the transition of No 44 Sqn from Hampdens, all subsequent new Lancaster units had converted from the Manchester. The latter type had made its final operational appearance against Bremen on 25/26 June, and this allowed the last unit, No 49 Sqn, to convert to the Lancaster.

No IX Sqn was the first Wellington unit to convert to the Lancaster, moving from No 3 Group to No 5 Group to do so. In doing so, No IX Sqn effectively replaced one of the Hampden units (Nos 144 and 489 Sqns) from the group, which had transferred to Coastal Command earlier in the year. No 57 Sqn followed No IX over from No 3 Group the following month. This brought No 5 Group up to a strength of ten Lancaster squadrons, and although it would later gain five new Lancaster units, these squadrons marked an expansion of the group, rather than conversion of its existing units.

The next Lancaster units to convert would therefore be from No 1 Group, the next priority to convert, and the only one of the night bomber groups not already equipping with four-engined heavies. No 3 Group, for example, was already well advanced in the process of conversion to the Stirling, while No 4 Group was well on the way towards becoming an all-Halifax group.

September 1942 was in many respects a disappointing month, starting out with a 231-aircraft attack against Saarbrücken on 1/2 September which entirely missed the target and instead devastated the smaller rural town of Saarlouis, 15 miles away.

Loss rates continued to hover around the 'unsustainable' four per cent level, occasionally rising very much higher, and the improvement in accuracy was patchy. Highlights were 251- and 446-aircraft raids

Issued to No 50 Sqn in June 1942, B I R5689/VN-N spent its entire (brief) life with this unit. The aircraft was lost on 19 September 1942 when it crashed on landing at Thurlby after a 'gardening sortie' to Nasturtium, killing four of its crew (including the pilot, Flg Off G W M Harrison). It is seen here taxiing out to the runway at Skellingthorpe earlier that year
(*via Bruce Robertson*)

against Bremen on 4/5 and 13/14 September, a 479-aircraft raid against Düsseldorf on 10/11 September and a 202-aircraft raid against Wilhelmshaven on 16/17 September. Other attacks were less successful, with more scattered bombing.

The first of the two attacks against Bremen saw the Pathfinders split between 'illuminators', who lit up the target area with white flares, 'visual markers' who dropped coloured flares on the aim point and 'backers up' who dropped incendiaries on these marked aim points. The raid caused heavy damage and 124 people were killed, although with 12 aircraft lost, including a Lancaster, the result was a costly one.

The Pathfinders used their new 'Pink Pansies' for the first time during the attack against Düsseldorf, which seemed to bring about greater accuracy, although with a 7.1 per cent loss rate, including five Lancasters and no less than 20 Wellingtons, the Command was continuing down the road to complete annihilation. Nor was Düsseldorf an exception – a much less accurate raid against Essen on 16/17 September resulted in a loss rate of 10.6 per cent.

The Wilhelmshaven raid (which saw the last use of the Hampden by Bomber Command) was more successful, with accurate bombing and the loss of only two Wellingtons.

On 23/24 September a small all-Lancaster raid numbering 83 aircraft was mounted by No 5 Group on the town of Wismar and the nearby Dornier factory. Major damage and heavy casualties were inflicted, but four aircraft were lost. These brought September's total Lancaster losses to 33 – two squadrons' worth of a ten-squadron force.

October saw the conversion of three No 1 Group Wellington and Halifax units to the Lancaster, these being Nos 101, 103 and 460 Sqns. In recent months (and especially after the retirement of the Manchester), the elderly Wellingtons had been suffering by far the worst loss rate of Bomber Command's remaining night bombers, and replacing them was of the highest priority. With plans for an all-Canadian No 6 Group well underway, the long term intention was for Nos 1, 3 and 5 Groups to operate the Lancaster, and for Nos 4 and 6 to operate the Halifax. No 3 Group was already dominated by the Stirling, so No 1 Group was the natural choice to re-equip next.

Another shot of R5689, but this time on the wing. This aircraft is typical of early B Is, with its row of fuselage windows. Although only a matter of weeks old when this photograph was taken, R5689 already has heavy exhaust staining over the uppersurfaces of its wings. No 50 Sqn was Bomber Command's sixth Lancaster unit, flying its first operation from Skellingthorpe on 30 May 1942 (*via Bruce Robertson*)

An evocative photo of a Lancaster running up prior to take off sometime in 1942. Night after night Bomber Command sent out fleets of bombers in an initially vain attempt to destroy German industry and the morale of its industrial workers. The effect on British morale was more obvious, giving the hard-pressed nation the feeling that it was, at last, hitting back at the hated Hun! (*via Francis K Mason*)

Eighteen Lancasters were lost during October (another squadron's worth), and the apparent improvement by comparison with September probably reflected the lower intensity of operations as much as an underlying, but slight improvement in loss rates.

Accuracy remained at best patchy, and at worst very poor. An attack on Köln by 289 aircraft (18 of which failed to return) was carefully assessed and catalogued by the city's efficient bureaucrats, who counted one '*Luftmine*' (4000-lb bomb), three HE bombs and 210 incendiaries as having fallen on the city, injuring four residents and seriously damaging two houses. The remainder fell away from the target, many on an effective decoy – some 71 4000-lb bombs, 231 smaller HE bombs and 68,590 incendiaries were dropped. The highlight of the month for the Lancasters was the Le Creusot raid, described in Chapter Three.

Sixteen Lancasters failed to return during the month of November (representing another squadron of aircraft) despite the onset of winter weather, and an inevitable slackening off of the offensive. Bomber Command switched some of the focus of its offensive away from Germany and against Italy, sending four major raids across the Alps to Genoa, and four more to Turin. On 28/29 November, Guy Gibson and another No 106 Sqn crew each took an 8000-lb bomb over the Alps to Turin. Apart from these attacks, the only large-scale raids were made against Hamburg and Stuttgart. Losses on the Italian missions were very low, with three 'no loss' attacks.

The raid on Hamburg on 9/10 November was frustrated by poor weather, and casualties and damage on the ground was light. However, 15 of the 213 aircraft sent out failed to return (a 7.5 per cent loss rate), including five Lancasters.

Two more units converted to the Lancaster during November, one being No 1 Group Wellington unit No 12 Sqn, the other being a newly-forming Australian-manned outfit within No 5 Group, No 467 Sqn. The latter effectively replaced No 83 Sqn, which had transferred to the Pathfinders in August, bringing No 5 Group back up to a strength of ten frontline Lancaster units.

In December the campaign against Turin continued, and major raids also struck at Duisburg, Frankfurt, Mannheim and Munich. The month also saw the loss of 26 Lancasters. Results against the German targets were disappointing, with very few bombs hitting the cities against which they were aimed, and with an average loss rate of more than five per cent. The three attacks against Turin were altogether more successful, with a high degree of accuracy, considerable damage to the target and relatively light losses.

The attack on Munich on 21/22 December did afford some opportunities for heroism, and the wireless operator of one No 83 Sqn Lancaster, Flt Sgt Leslie Wallace RNZAF, was decorated for bravery. Despite being wounded in the leg, Wallace fought the fires in the burning aircraft, jettisoning burning material through the rear turret and eventually putting the blaze out. He then navigated the aircraft home, assisting his pilot to return to base without further incident.

The night of 4/5 June 1942 had marked the exact mid-point of the war. Despite the improvements introduced to service under Harris, the loss rate had continued to rise inexorably, while accuracy continued to give cause for concern, and it was estimated that between half and three-quarters of all bombs dropped were not hitting the cities which they were aimed at! But although half the war had passed, Bomber Command had barely 'got into its stride', and its offensive would step up considerably, with 82 per cent of its sorties and 94 per cent of its bomb tonnage yet to come, as well as 77 per cent of its losses. Put another way, delivering the first six per cent of its bombs had cost Bomber Command 23 per cent of its wartime losses, and totalled 18 per cent of its sorties. By the end of the year, little had really changed.

But the real lessons of 1942 remained largely unlearned. Bomber Command's night offensive had cost it dear, while causing little real damage to Germany. Again and again, large formations went out only to find the vast majority missing their (city-sized) targets. Aircrew casualties often outnumbered the deaths of German civilians.

Meanwhile, No 2 Group, derided as a side-show by Harris, regularly despatched squadron-strength raids by Douglas Bostons, most of which suffered no losses, and many of which saw extremely accurate bombing, although they carried relatively tiny bombloads, and tended to hit semi-tactical targets, although they could not range far into Germany itself. But it is doubtful whether the Lancaster and its like caused anything like as much damage and trouble to the Germans in 1942 as did the Boston, Mitchell and even the Blenheim – and that is without counting the contribution of No 2 Group's 'star performer', the de Havilland Mosquito.

But things were looking up. The Lancaster was proving to be in a class of its own, well ahead of the RAF's other night bombers, and by the end of the year Bomber Command had fifteen squadrons of these superb aircraft, ten of them fully equipping No 5 Group.

While the Great War had been largely fought between soldiers with bullet and bayonet, World War 2 was total war, involving civilians and servicemen alike, and it was fought with high tech weapons of massive destructive power. This load of Small Bomb Carriers (each containing up to 235 4-lb incendiaries) were Bomber Command's equivalent to the infantryman's 'Cold Steel', hated and feared in equal measure by the enemy (*via Francis K Mason*)

LOW LEVEL AND BY DAYLIGHT

'If you want to find examples of ill-conceived, poorly-planned and badly-executed missions, you need look no further than Augsburg', said Sqn Ldr 'Charles M', a Lancaster pilot who flew on the Peenemünde raid later in the war. 'If a raid failed militarily, then the propagandists emphasised the courage and glory, awarding a VC here and a DSO or two there. If it succeeded, the medal count was rather more modest, and they stressed the military effect. You only have to look at Garland and Grey and the Meuse bridges, Scarff in the Far East, Nettleton at Augsburg, Gibson and the dams and poor old Hugh Malcolm in his Blenheim – military cock-ups all of them, and missions that should never have been authorised, and which wasted the lives of some fine men'.

Preparations for the Augsburg raid began at a very early stage in the Lancaster's career, with a series of low level training flights by Nos 44 and 97 Sqns, the RAF's first Lancaster units. Neither knew what the other was doing, and the two squadrons were not brought together until the raid itself, even briefing separately at their respective bases. These training flights (inevitably culminating in a mock attack against a coastal target) led many aircrew to expect that they would be ordered to attack Kiel, so that when they were briefed on the morning of 17 April 1942, there was an air of astonishment and disbelief.

Route tapes stretched across the massive briefing room maps, crossed the Channel at Le Havre and ran south to a point below Paris, where they turned east close to Sens. Skimming the Swiss border, the tapes stretched towards the Ammer See and Munich, but they turned north to Augsburg and the MAN diesel engine factory. This was a long haul by any standards, and meandered through the heart of enemy-held Europe. Moreover, the Lancaster crews would be expected to fly their mission at low level and by day. Many predicted that the elaborately planned diversionary attacks by 30 Bostons and some 700 fighter sorties might not be enough to keep the Luftwaffe from intervening, and most privately viewed the raid as being dangerously close to a suicide mission.

It is safe to assume that such thoughts did not cross the mind of

Sqn Ldr John Nettleton (left) led the Augsburg raid, being the captain of the sole No 44 Sqn Lancaster to return from the mission. He is seen here after the raid with fellow No 44 Sqn Flight Commander, Sqn Ldr Whitehead (*via Francis K Mason*)

the raid's leader, the charismatic acting CO of No 44 Sqn, Sqn Ldr John Dering Nettleton. Like Fighter Command's Malan, Nettleton was a tough South African, a 'Botha Boy' who had served as a naval cadet on the same South African Training Ship, *General Botha*, as the Spitfire ace, and who had also served in the South African Merchant Marine. Nettleton had been commissioned in the RAF in December 1938, and flew with Nos 207, 98, and

185 Sqns before joining No 44, then flying Hampdens. By the time of the Augsburg raid, this unit was commanded by Wg Cdr Roderick Learoyd VC, but the latter officer had barely converted onto the Lancaster, leaving the fearless Nettleton to lead the mission.

But whatever the thoughts of the crews, six Lancasters from each unit took off from Woodhall Spa and Waddington laden with the maximum fuel load of 1154 gallons and carrying four 1000-lb bombs, each with an 11-second delay detonator. These made their rendezvous before flying across the Channel at barely 50 ft, the six No 44 Sqn B Is (led by Sqn Ldr J D Nettleton) leading the six No 97 Sqn Lancasters (led by Sqn Ldr J S Sherwood) offset three miles to starboard.

Unfortunately, someone rescheduled the elaborately planned diversionary operation, and the Bostons served only to draw enemy fighters into the air and into the path of the Lancaster force. *Stab* and II./JG 2 scrambled a full *Gruppe* of Fw 190s after the six bombers literally overflew the unit's airfield at Beaumont-le-Roger. These quickly caught up with Nettleton's formation and began to fight an hour-long running battle which saw all three aircraft in the second section shot down.

One aircraft was claimed by Unteroffizier Pohl in his Fw 190A-2, and this became the unit's 1000th victory of the war. His victim, Wt Off H V Crum DFM, force-landed L7548 successfully in a wheatfield, and his crew all survived to become PoWs, but the other two aircraft were lost with all hands. The German fighters then downed one aircraft from the first section (flown by Sgt G T Rhodes) and scored hits on the remaining two, before pulling back short of fuel.

The surviving No 44 Sqn Lancasters (R5508, flown by Nettleton, and Flg Off A J Garwell DFM in R5510) pressed on and attacked the

This trio of No 44 Sqn Lancasters served with the unit's conversion flight, as shown by the bars above their individual code letters. The Augsburg raid was based around the use of vics of three aircraft (*Aerospace Publishing*)

R5740 was among No 44 Sqn's earliest Lancasters, but it did not participate in the Augsburg mission. The B I survived until 25/26 June 1943, when it was posted missing during a mission to Gelsenkirchen (*via Francis K Mason*)

Although this B I wears the same code-letters as the aircraft flown by Sqn Ldr Nettleton on the Augsburg raid, it is not the Lancaster that he used on this mission. This particular machine, which is even being flown by the VC winner in this photograph, was captured on film in February 1944. Although assigned to No 44 Sqn, L7578 was used by No 97 Sqn for conversion training, and it spent much of its life flying with a succession of training units (*via Francis K Mason*)

factory, although Garwell's aircraft was badly hit and crash-landed, with the loss of three crew-members.

Sherwood's formation, meanwhile, had fallen behind, having set a slower speed in order to conserve precious fuel. Fortunately, they had been ignored by the Fw 190s and Bf 109s as they streamed back towards their base, and arrived at the target about four minutes later. Sherwood's aircraft (L7573) crashed as it pulled off the target, as did a machine in the second No 97 Sqn section, which was set alight and exploded immediately after dropping its bombs, but the remaining four aircraft escaped, returning safely to base as darkness fell. Remarkably, Sherwood escaped death, being hurled (still strapped into his armoured seat) into conifers, which cushioned his fall.

One of the surviving No 97 Sqn aircraft had been set alight over the target, and it limped home on three engines, only to be declared a total write-off the next morning. But four B Is and their crews (of six) had returned to Woodhall Spa. At Waddington, Sqn Ldr Nettleton and his crew returned alone, having lost all five of their wingmen.

Some 12 of the 17 bombs dropped (and of the 48 carried by the 12 aircraft) actually exploded, and these caused heavy damage to a small part of the factory (destroying three per cent of its machine tools), while the raid provided a spectacular 'feat of arms' for the British people. The attack was also presented as marking a stark demonstration of Bomber Command's ability to hit outlying areas of Germany, although in truth it was no more than a pin-prick, achieving little impact on production at the MAN plant.

Nettleton received the VC for his 'unflinching determination, leadership and valour of the highest order'. But other factories made up the shortfall in production of diesel engines, and tank and U-boat output was barely affected.

Nos 44 and 97 Sqns each despatched six Lancasters on the Augsburg raid, in two vics of three. Four of No 44's aircraft were shot down by fighters en route to the target, where another fell, but No 97 Sqn fared better, losing only two of its Lancasters. Built alongside a number of the aircraft that participated in the daring mission, this machine, L7583, was issued to No 207 Sqn in April 1942. Serving with the unit until March of the following year, its remaining time in the RAF was spent with No 1661 HCU and No 5 Lancaster Finishing School. L7583 was scrapped on 31 November 1946
(*Aerospace Publishing*)

No 97 Sqn's Lancasters were relatively seldom photographed, and carried unusually narrow code letters, as seen here on the rear fuselage section of R5482. This aircraft flew No 97's first Lancaster op, and after the incident which resulted in this damage, it was repaired and issued to No 101 Sqn – flying that unit's first Lancaster operation, too! R5482 was written off when it crashed on landing at the unit's Holme-on-Spalding Moor base on 10 December 1942
(*via Francis K Mason*)

A raid against Le Havre's power station and docks by 12 Bostons the previous day perhaps marked the type of operation that Bomber Command should have been concentrating on. This had seen every bomb fall on the target, and all 12 Bostons return to base without loss, while 12 more had achieved the same result against Mondeville power station on 14 April. But this sort of result was entirely routine for the Bostons, and went largely unremarked by the propagandists.

Unescorted daylight raids by heavy bombers had proved unacceptably costly at the beginning of the war, although low level flying had been shown to afford some sanctuary for the faster light and medium bombers like the Boston, which Harris despised as an irrelevance due to its lack of range and payload. Against this background, the fact that the Augsburg raid was ever authorised at all was astonishing, as was Harris's lack of protest at a venture which would surely have counted as one of the 'diversions, adventures and stunts' which he despised, and which threatened the build-up of his precious heavy bomber force.

Nor was Harris (a convinced adherent of the Trenchardian doctrine of the 'moral', psychological effect of area bombing) particularly well disposed towards pinpoint attacks against specific factories. Yet while one might have expected Harris to use the heavy losses to justify his opposition to such missions, he actually seems to have greeted the raid with enthusiasm, and as having demonstrated the effectiveness of the new Lancaster! He even defended the raid against criticism by the Ministry of Economic Warfare, who complained to Churchill and the Air Ministry that other bottleneck targets in southern Germany were more of a priority than the MAN works.

Even more remarkably, the Augsburg raid formed the blueprint for another two successively larger daylight raids in July and October 1942. On each occasion, though, the Lancasters would meet with greater success and better luck.

The first of these follow-up attacks was mounted on 11 July against the U-boat yards at Danzig – the most distant target yet attempted by Bomber Command. Some 44 Lancasters sortied, flying out over the North Sea at low level

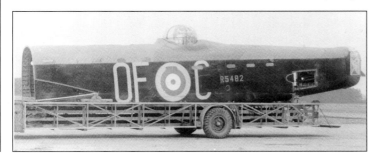

and in formation. The aircraft then split up and flew to the target independently, taking advantage of cloud cover over Denmark and the Baltic. The 'heavies' bombed from 'normal height' as dusk fell, then returned to England in darkness. Twenty-four Lancasters had bombed the target, and two more were shot down in the target area.

When Harris received orders to attack the French Schneider armament factory at Le Creusot, it presented him with a problem. While he had little compunction against inflicting civilian casualties while attacking German targets, Harris was naturally concerned about collateral damage when attacking targets in occupied France. The Pathfinders (whose formation is described in Chapter Five) were not yet accurate enough to ensure the degree of precision required, and Harris reluctantly accepted that the only option would be a set-piece daylight raid by low-flying Lancasters.

Following the example of Augsburg, the decision was taken to launch the raid in the early afternoon, so that the force would bomb in daylight (to ensure accuracy), but which would then return to base under cover of darkness. Eight squadrons carried out a low level exercise over the Wash, with RAF Spitfires attempting to disrupt their aim, on 1 October. Nine units offered a total of 94 Lancasters for the raid itself on 17 October. These rendezvoused over Upper Heyford before setting out for France in a great gaggle, staying below 1000 ft in order to avoid detection by enemy radar. The Lancasters, led by Wg Cdr Leonard Slee of No 49 Sqn, crossed the French coast at 300 ft close to Nantes, and looped around Tours en route to the target.

Nearing the target, the nine squadrons (only five aircraft having turned back early) fanned out and climbed to 4000 ft for their bombing runs, while six aircraft (two each from Nos 106, 9 and 61 Sqns, led by Wg Cdr Guy Gibson) pushed on to bomb the Henri Paul transformer station at Montchanin, six miles further south. These aircraft attacked in line astern from a nominal 500 ft, although Hopgood's aircraft was damaged by the blast from his own bombs at 150 ft and Corr's aircraft crashed in the target area, almost certainly due to the same cause.

A gaggle of at least 47 Lancasters (of a total force of 88 aircraft!) roar over the riverside town of Mon Richard, en route to Schneider's Le Creusot works. This raid was to be a stunning success for low level bombing, following the gallant failure at Augsburg (*Aerospace Publishing*)

Another B I (from No 57 Sqn) was damaged when it flushed out a covey of partridges on the return trip, several of the birds smashing the windscreen and injuring the flight engineer. But apart from Corr's machine, all aircraft returned home safely.

In assigning a code-name to the operation, someone had ignored the British convention of not using a word with any connection to the target or mission, and used the name *Robinson* (Robinson Creusot!). This had, however, proved to be lucky, for of the 94 Lancasters despatched by Bomber Command on Operation *Robinson*, only one was lost, although several more were damaged and three crew-members were injured, one fatally. One photo-reconnaissance Spitfire was lost, along with its pilot, during efforts to obtain post-mission photography, but it was eventually established that the plant was put out of action completely for more than three weeks, while repair work disrupted production for more than eight months.

But the success of Operation *Robinson* was not sufficient to persuade Harris that there was any real place for day-bombing, either by his growing force of 'heavies' or even by the medium bombers, and No 2 Group's star continued to wane.

A post-strike photograph showing extensive damage to the Breuil Steelworks at Le Creusot. The general machine shops (bottom) were straddled by a stick of 1000-lb bombs, the steel manufacturing plant and sheet and bar mills badly hit and a 650-ft warehouse entirely destroyed (*via Bruce Robertson*)

This reconnaissance photograph shows further damage at Le Creusot, where many buildings were destroyed by direct hits. These are the processing works and locomotive machine shop (*via Francis K Mason*)

COLOUR PLATES

1
Lancaster B III EE129/MG-Y of No 7 Sqn, No 8 (PFF) Group, Oakington, Autumn 1943

2
Lancaster B III ED480/WS-U of No IX Sqn, Waddington, February 1943

3
Lancaster B III JA852/WS-L of No IX Sqn, Bardney, July 1943

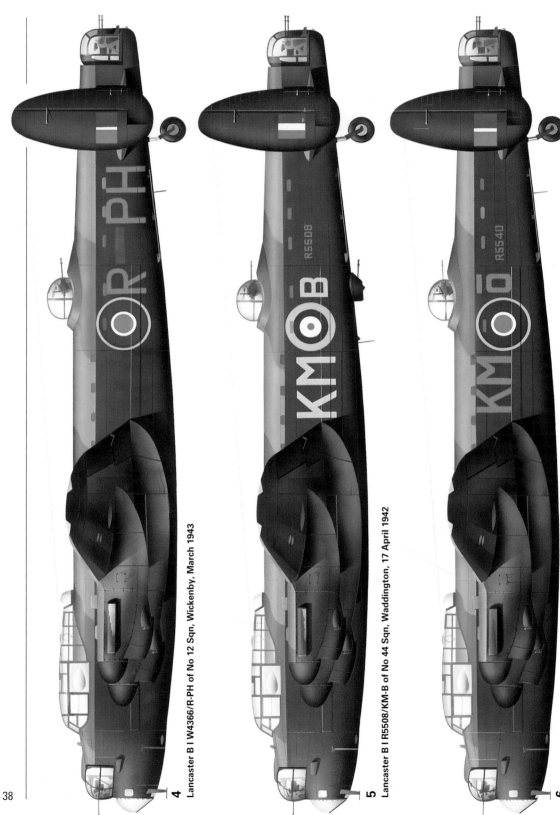

4

Lancaster B I W4366/R-PH of No 12 Sqn, Wickenby, March 1943

5

Lancaster B I R5508/KM-B of No 44 Sqn, Waddington, 17 April 1942

6

Lancaster B I R5540/KM-O of No 44 Sqn's conversion flight, Waddington, 29 September 1942

7

Lancaster B I W4110/KM-K of No 44 Sqn, Waddington, March 1943

8

Lancaster B III ED702/EA-D of No 49 Sqn, Fiskerton, March 1943

9

Lancaster B I R5702/VN-S of No 50 Sqn, Swinderby, October 1942

10 Lancaster B III ED828/VN-S of No 50 Sqn, Skellingthorpe, Spring 1943

11 Lancaster B III ED989/DX-F of No 57 Sqn, Scampton, 27 May 1943

12 Lancaster B II DS604/QR-W of No 61 Sqn, Syerston, January 1943

13
Lancaster B III LM360/QR-O of No 61 Sqn, Skellingthorpe, 3/4 November 1943

14
Lancaster B I R5669/OL-E of No 83 Sqn, Scampton, Summer 1942

15
Lancaster B I L7571/OF-X of No 97 Sqn, Woodhall Spa, March 1942

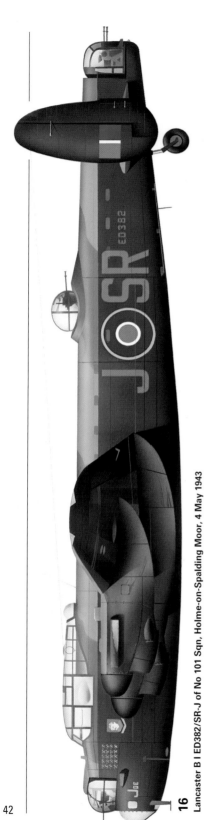

16 Lancaster B I ED382/SR-J of No 101 Sqn, Holme-on-Spalding Moor, 4 May 1943

17 Lancaster B III ED905/PM-X of No 103 Sqn, Elsham Wolds, May 1943

18 Lancaster B I R5677/ZN-A of No 106 Sqn, Coningsby, September 1942

19

Lancaster B I W4118/ZN-Y of No 106 Sqn, Syerston, November 1942

20

Lancaster B II DS685/KO-A of No 115 Sqn, Little Snoring, August 1943

21

Lancaster B I W4851/GT-E of No 156 Sqn, No 8 (PFF) Group, Warboys, April 1943

43

22 Lancaster B III ED905/AS-X of No 166 Sqn, Kirmington, September 1943

23 Lancaster B I R5570/EM-F of No 207 Sqn, Bottesford, May 1942

24 Lancaster B X KB700/LQ-Q of No 405 Sqn, Gransden Lodge, November 1943

25

Lancaster B II DS708/OW-Q of No 426 Sqn, Linton-on-Ouse, November 1943

26

Lancaster B II DS689/OW-S of No 426 Sqn, Linton-on-Ouse, September 1943

27

Lancaster B III JB607/AR-N of No 460 Sqn, Binbrook, Winter 1943

46

28 Lancaster B III ED539/PO-V of No 467 Sqn, Bottesford, Summer 1943

29 Lancaster B IS ED912/G/AJ-S of No 617 Sqn, Coningsby, December 1943

30 Lancaster B X CF-CMS (ex-B I R5727), Canadian TransAtlantic Air Service, late 1943

SHIP-BUSTING

The lack of priority accorded to the re-equipment of Coastal Command led to an unfulfilled appetite for air power by the Admiralty. As the RAF's principal operator of long range aircraft, Bomber Command was frequently called upon to augment Coastal Command's own meagre assets. It probably did not help that maritime operations had been Bomber Command's lot during the earliest months of the war, while attacks on mainland targets were effectively prohibited. With little else to do, Bomber Command was sent out against naval shipping and harbour installations, raising expectations that it would continue to do so.

From an early stage in its operational career, the Lancaster was used for coastal minelaying (amassing some 2929 minelaying or 'Gardening' sorties by war's end), and such sorties formed a significant proportion of No 44 Sqn's early missions. Even when despatched on bombing missions, many of the targets were coastal towns, or towns which lay close inland.

In April 1942, both Nos 44 and 97 Sqns mounted seven-aircraft detachments to RAF Lossiemouth, near Elgin, which was a Bomber Command No 6 Group airfield housing the Wellingtons of No 20 OTU. On 27 April six aircraft from each unit were despatched to attack *Tirpitz* as it lay at anchor at Trondheim. Few aircraft even sighted the target on their first run, and a second pass brought no success. Only 11 Lancasters returned from the mission, and four of 31 Halifaxes despatched against the same target also failed to return. A second attempt the following night was no more successful.

When America finally entered the war following the Japanese attack on Pearl Harbor on 7 December 1941, the U-boat packs briefly turned their attentions to US coastal waters, where they enjoyed a 230,000 ton, 40-ship orgy of destruction in just three weeks. But despite this diversion, and the permanent retention of 24 U-boats off Norway in preparation for a feared invasion, losses of Allied ships in the Atlantic (although reduced) continued to be a source of great concern.

Coastal Command's AOC-in-C, Air Chief Marshal Sir Philip Joubert, was convinced that Britain could not survive for more than a year unless shipping losses were staunched, and that in order to halt

A No 61 Sqn crew walk out to their Lancaster. Several Bomber Command Lancaster units were temporarily attached to Coastal Command during 1942 including No 61 Sqn, which sent eight aircraft and twelve crews to RAF St Eval, in Cornwall, on 16 July for a five-week period, scoring a U-boat kill on the first sortie! The Lancasters proved unreliable, and three failed to return on 19 August, and another the next day. Harris was furious at the loss of four aircraft and 28 aircrew, while achieving 'only' the destruction of a single U-boat (*via Bruce Robertson*)

Wg Cdr Guy Gibson DFC (centre, hands in pockets) and the crews of No 106 Sqn are seen at Coningsby on 31 May 1942 after their participation in the first Thousand Bomber Raid. They could also be celebrating the news that their awful Manchesters (both a B I and IA are visible behind the group) were on the verge of being replaced by Lancasters – the unit completed its conversion the following month. At 24, their CO, Guy Gibson, was one of the youngest squadron commanders in Bomber Command, having taking over No 106 Sqn from Wg Cdr Robert Swinton Allen in March 1942. A vastly experienced pilot, he had previously flown Hampdens with No 83 Sqn and Beaufighters with No 29 Sqn (*Aerospace Publishing*)

the flow, his Command would require more aircraft.

In fact, Japan's entry into the war initially weakened home-based Coastal Command, with the despatch of Catalina units overseas. Rivalries between Coastal and Bomber Commands dated back to the beginning of the war, and Joubert's predecessor, 'Ginger' Bowhill, had fought 'tooth and nail' with Sir Richard Peirse (Harris' precursor) in order to obtain the assets he needed to effectively fight the Battle of the Atlantic. Desperately short of Sunderland flying boats and long-range four-engined aircraft, Coastal Command was forced to rely on a handful of Bomber Command's obsolete cast-off Whitleys and Wellingtons, and it had to fight hard to retain even these.

Senior officers at Bomber Command regarded Coastal Command's Atlantic battle as an irrelevant side-show, although in retrospect, and taking into account the miserable accuracy figures being obtained by Bomber Command, it seems likely that an aircraft assigned to Coastal Command was making a more valuable contribution than one serving with Bomber Command.

'Coastal Command was mauling enemy shipping, while simultaneously hitting the expensively produced U-boats and enforcing a blockade on Germany which imposed huge cost and inconvenience on German industry and the German people. Bomber Command was scattering bombs over the German countryside, killing the odd cow!', claimed a Whitley pilot who flew with both Commands. Post-war research backs him up, indicating that even after bombing accuracy improved, a four-engined aircraft assigned to Coastal Command imposed 20 times more damage on the German economy than a similar machine serving with Bomber Command. But this was far from clear at the time.

At the beginning of 1942 Joubert demanded the immediate transfer of six Wellington squadrons, with the provision of 81 Liberators and/or Fortresses in the longer term. Bomber Command was tardy in responding to the demand, and released only a few worn-out Whitleys. Meanwhile, the U-boats began to improve their kill/loss ratio, and spent more time in the mid-Atlantic, out of range of all but the Liberators of No 120 Sqn. This made it even more important to interdict the U-boats as they transited the Bay of Biscay, and for Bomber Command aircraft to protect shipping close to the coast, thus freeing up all available Coastal Command aircraft for longer range missions.

By withholding the four-engined aircraft which Coastal Command so badly needed, Peirse and Harris made it inevitable that they would lose aircraft (including Lancasters) and their crews on temporary attachment to Coastal Command. In June 1942, Bomber Command temporarily lost half of the longest-serving and most experienced of its seven Lancaster units when five No 44 Sqn Lancasters were detached to Nutts Corner in County Antrim, Northern Ireland, for the second half of the month. The detachment attacked two submarines during its brief stint, with Flt Lt T P C Barlow DFC sinking the second.

The next Bomber Command Lancaster unit attached to Coastal Command was No 61 Sqn, which sent eight aircraft and twelve crews to RAF St Eval, in Cornwall, on 16 July for a five-week period. Remarkably, the unit scored its first U-boat kill on the first sortie flown from St Eval, but claimed no further successes. The Lancasters began to show worrying signs of unreliability, however, and suffered several engine failures. Finally, on 19 August, three of the unit's Lancasters failed to return from sorties against the *Corunna*, a German blockade runner, and one more was damaged by flak. No 50 Sqn joined the cat and mouse game with the *Corunna* the next day, when No 61 Sqn lost a fourth aircraft.

Harris used this episode to justify his opposition to the 'diversion' of resources to 'irrelevant side-shows', pointing out that 12 No 61 Sqn had mounted 96 patrols, totalling 878 hours, with the loss of four aircraft and 28 aircrew, while achieving 'only' the destruction of a single U-boat. Whether a month's normal operations would have achieved anything greater remains uncertain, although this was Harris's unspoken assumption.

Bomber Command's record against the Kriegsmarine was poor up to that point in the war, having failed to stop the battleships *Scharnhorst* and *Gneisenau*, and the battlecruiser *Prinz Eugen*, as they escaped in the infamous 'Channel Dash' on 12 February 1942, and had inflicted little damage on the *Tirpitz* in its Norwegian lair, despite making numerous attempts to sink it. Part of the problem was the lack of suitable weapons, although various establishments had been working on a range of possible solutions to the problem for some months.

No 106 Sqn's strength included several Royal Navy officers (three are visible in this photo of the unit's aircrew), reflecting the unit's secondary maritime commitment. Indeed, these men were attached to the unit at the time it was working up with the Capital Ship Bomb in August 1942. The fourth individual in a dark blue uniform is an RAAF navigator – Australian crewmen served with virtually all Bomber Command units (*via Francis K Mason*)

This No 106 Sqn Lancaster has extremely heavily stained engine cowlings, and features a two-row bomb log and nickname (possibly *HERE'S HOWIE!*) below the cockpit. The ventral H_2S radome marks it out as being with the unit after Guy Gibson's period as Officer Commanding (*via Francis K Mason*)

No 106 Sqn's Lancasters made a number of daring daylight attacks against enemy ships and harbour facilities, including several using the fatally inaccurate Capital Ship Bomb, which was delivered from altitudes which virtually guaranteed a miss! (*via Francis K Mason*)

The most promising (and most advanced) of these was the so-called Capital Ship Bomb, a 5600-lb monster with a hollow (shaped) charge warhead. This was described as looking 'like an elongated turnip', and it was intended to penetrate an armoured deck before exploding and blowing out the ship's bottom. The most alarming German warship, in the eyes of the Admiralty was the aircraft carrier *Graf Zeppelin*, nearing completion in the Polish port of Gdynia, where the ships involved in the 'Channel Dash' were also believed to be 'holed up'.

Gdynia thus became the natural target for the first, and only, raid using the new Capital Ship Bombs, four of which had by then been constructed. Bomber Command detailed Wg Cdr Guy Gibson's No 106 Sqn to carry out the mission, ordering six crews to begin training for the then-still unspecified operation, and directing that six aircraft should be modified to carry the weapon. The new bombs were incredibly expensive and difficult to produce, and one was used for ballistics trials, which showed that it had an extremely irregular and unpredictable trajectory, which would make accurate aiming all but impossible, except from very low level. In this context, even 1000 ft was regarded as being too high!

It was at this point that the attempt to use the weapon was doomed to failure. It was decided that dropping the new weapons from 1000 ft would entail an unacceptable degree of risk to the Lancaster crews, and the decision was taken to bomb from 6000 ft. On the night of 26/27 July 1942, three No 106 Sqn Lancasters, captained by Gibson, Whamond and Hopgood, were despatched against Gdynia, which they found covered by a veil of haze and mist.

They remained in the target area for about one hour, despite heavy flak, and caught fleeting glimpses of two capital ships. After about a dozen bombing runs, all three aircraft had dropped their weapons, but all missed – Gibson's by a reported 400 yards. The aircraft involved in the raid had staggered into the air at an unprecedented all up weight of 67,000 lbs, an astonishing 7000 lbs above the aircraft's authorised

Maximum Take Off Weight. Some sources suggest that No 106 despatched nine Lancasters, and that each carried one of the new bombs, but this cannot be confirmed.

The modifications to the six No 106 Sqn B Is also allowed them to carry the new 8000-lb HC (High Capacity) bomb, and the unit began operations with it on 31 July/1 August, initially against Düsseldorf, and later carrying the weapons to Nuremberg and to Turin.

The Lancaster's ability to carry very large bombs has often been cited as being the type's main advantage over its rivals. But interestingly, Wt Off P E Merrals, historic trip to Düsseldorf on 31 July was not the first occasion on which an 8000-lb HC bomb had been dropped. That honour went to Plt Off M W Renault of No 76 Sqn, who dropped one on Essen on 10/11 April 1942 from his Halifax. Unlike poor Merrals, Renault survived his operation, and returned to base to describe his success. Doubt still exists as to whether Merrals and his crew were shot down before or after they had dropped their bomb.

It has been intimated that No 106 Sqn would, and should, have been No 5 Group's contribution to the Pathfinders, but that this did not happen either because a run of special operations had allowed No 83 Sqn to briefly slip past No 106 to reach the top of the Group bombing ladder, or even because Air Marshal Coryton (AOC No 5 Group) would not countenance losing his 'best' squadron. Others believe that the best unit won, pointing out that No 106 Sqn had customarily been between fifth and seventh on the bombing ladder.

'Don Bennett was no fool, and I think that he felt that missing a battleship by 400 yards (400 yards!) from 6000 ft wasn't the degree of accuracy he wanted for the Pathfinders, and that he wanted No 83 Sqn in preference to No 106. I don't mean any disrespect to Gibson, but his was *one* of the best units in the Group, and force of personality and a flair for publicity shouldn't be allowed to alter that fact. You should remember that when the Pathfinders needed a second unit from No 5 Group, No 106 was again passed over, and that No 97 was chosen instead', commented a veteran Lancaster pilot from No 5 Group.

But while Gibson and No 106 Sqn were not selected for transfer to the Pathfinders, they would form the basis of the most famous RAF bomber unit of all time – No 617 Sqn, described in Chapter Seven.

During December 1942, there were discussions at HQ No 5 Group about the possibility of forming a special unit for 'out-of-the-ordinary' operations, and some have suggested that the AOC's preferred solution would have been to assign this role to Gibson's No 106 Sqn. There have been suggestions that Gibson himself felt that this would have required staffing the unit with hand-picked experienced crews, with no inexperienced first-tourists. In the event, No 106 Sqn remained 'just another Main Force bomber squadron', but the idea of a special unit was destined not to die there.

The Capital Ship Bomb was expensive and difficult to produce, and ballistics trials showed that the bluff-fronted bomb had an extremely irregular and unpredictable trajectory. This made accurate aiming all but impossible, except from very low level. In this context, even 1000 ft was regarded as being too high. Unfortunately 1000 ft was felt to entail an unacceptable degree of risk to No 106 Sqn's crews attacking targets heavily protected by flak batteries, and the decision was taken to bomb from 6000 ft (*via Francis K Mason*)

LANCASTER PATHFINDERS

Ironically, the innovation which did most to improve the accuracy of Bomber Command's strategic bombing offensive was copied from the Luftwaffe. During 1940, the Luftwaffe had formed a specialised 'pathfinder' unit whose Heinkels were flown by experienced crews, using advanced radio navigation aids to accurately mark targets for attacks by the 'Main Force'. The *Knickebein* equipment on which *Kampfgruppe* 100 relied was susceptible to jamming, and the pathfinder offensive soon flagged, but there can be no doubt as to its influence.

Initial attempts at using experienced, highly-skilled crews to find and mark targets dated back to the earliest phases of Bomber Command's offensive. One of the leading lights was Wg Cdr S O Bufton, who had pioneered the technique while leading Nos 10 and 76 Sqns, locating and marking the target by using flares, and then attracting other crews by the use of coloured Verey lights. As a group captain, Bufton became Director of Bomber Operations at the Air Ministry, and argued strongly that the most experienced and highly skilled crews (who had proved consistently best able to find and bomb their targets) might be gathered together to form an elite Target Finding Force.

The widespread use of the *Gee* pulse-phasing radar navaid allowed RAF bombers to operate with great accuracy over fairly short ranges, but was itself jammed from the summer of 1942. Discussions as to the need for and desirability of a dedicated, permanent British Target Finding Force (as raised by Bufton) continued during early 1942.

Harris agreed in principle with the need for target-marking, but profoundly opposed the formation of any *corps d'elite* within Bomber Command, preferring to keep the bomber 'aces' within their units where they could encourage, lead and inspire through example. He therefore preferred to assign one unit within each group to Target Finding duties each month, based on its success in the previous month's 'bombing ladder'. He felt that this would spread the load more fairly, would encourage an overall improvement in accuracy and would avoid bickering and jealousy.

Bufton believed that this was inadequate, and that dedicated

'Steady, steady . . .' Even Pathfinder aircrew admit to finding the wait for the magic words 'Bombs' Gone!' almost interminable. Although improving Bomber Command accuracy was a long-winded process, the results were eventually extremely impressive, thus allowing the Command to drop bombs with greater precision by night than the USAAF managed by day (*via Bruce Robertson*)

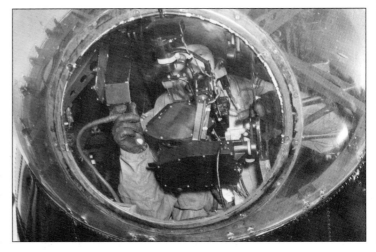

Unnecessary radio communication was avoided wherever possible, since it could forewarn Germany's defences of what was to come. Here, an airman signals take off clearance to a Wyton-based No 83 Sqn Lancaster using an Aldis lamp (*via Bruce Robertson*)

Don Bennett had hoped to be allocated a single squadron from each of Bomber Command's four groups, and that these squadrons would be new units, in turn formed from the best crews within each group. Instead, he won Harris' backing for a compromise, taking the unit which was then at the top of each groups' respective bombing ladder. No 5 Group provided the Lancaster-equipped No 83 Sqn, one of whose B Is is seen here (*Aerospace Publishing*)

Target Finder units would need to be permanently assigned to the role, allowing them to be able to exchange ideas and develop equipment, techniques and tactics.

Harris did not like the idea of forming single permanent Target Finder squadrons within the groups (let alone the idea of establishing a dedicated Force), and even when directly ordered to set aside two No 3 Group Wellington and two No 3 Group Stirling units for Target Finding, obstinately refused to skim off the best squadrons or crews for the purpose. He continued to argue that the widespread introduction of *Gee* and bomb cameras would enhance navigation accuracy and encourage competition, and that this would itself drive up bombing accuracy without dedicated target-finding. He further argued that if target finding was required, then the best way of assigning crews to the role was through constant competition.

Not far below the surface of the Target Finding argument lay the continuing struggle between the proponents of area bombing and those who wished to see a return to the accurate bombing of more selective targets. In the end, the increasing German jamming of *Gee* made the establishment of a dedicated Target Finder Force inevitable if the Main Force bombers were to be able to find even area targets.

When ordered to form the Force by the War Cabinet, Harris finally threw his weight behind the project with unexpected energy and enthusiasm, although he rejected the originally preferred Target Finding Force name in favour of the more evocative Pathfinder Force.

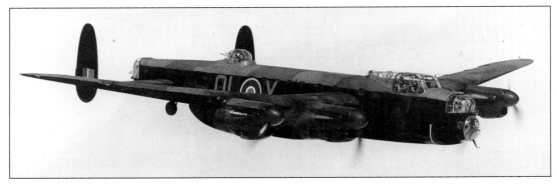

Harris even fought for Pathfinder crews to be promoted by one rank to compensate for their longer tours, and to make up for the more rapid promotion that these 'high fliers' might enjoy in normal squadrons.

Bufton pressed for the selection of the charismatic Grp Capt Basil Embry as the leader of the new Target Finding Force, but for reasons which remain unclear, he was passed over in favour of his Senior Air Staff Officer, the Australian Wg Cdr Don Bennett. Some sources suggest that Harris was responsible for the selection of Don Bennett as the Pathfinders' CO over the heads of Embry and other more senior men.

It should be remembered that while Bennett's pre-war experience pioneering long range routes with Imperial Airways had left him almost uniquely qualified as a long range navigator and pilot, he was a very junior wing commander, fresh from the command of a line Halifax squadron. Promoted to acting group captain in July 1942, he was given command of an organisation which would soon enjoy parity with other full sized groups, each of which was led by an air vice marshal! Bennett pushed for the permanent allocation of a squadron (preferably composed from the best crews from all that group's units) from each group to his Pathfinder Force, and won Harris's backing for taking the units which were then at the top of the groups' respective bombing ladders.

This arrangement saw the transfer of No 156 Sqn from No 1 Group (with Wellingtons), No 7 Sqn from No 3 Group (with Stirlings), No 35 Sqn from No 4 Group (with Halifaxes) and No 83 Sqn from No 5 Group (with Lancasters). These units moved to adjacent airfields within the No 3 Group area, No 83 Sqn finding itself at Wyton. The frontline groups were supposed to be responsible for supplying the Pathfinders with replacement crews (who, it was assumed, would be the best available), but only Air Vice Marshal Carr at No 4 Group fulfilled this obligation 'to the letter'.

The Pathfinder Force (PFF) was formally established on 15 August 1942, and it almost began operations within hours, for a mission was cancelled shortly before take off that same night – most of No 83's Lancasters had only arrived at their new home that very day.

After this false start, No 83 Sqn contributed six Lancasters to an attack on Flensburg. This proved to be something of a damp squib, and dramatically underlined the weakness of the PFF in poor weather using the equipment then available. It had been forecast that the weather would be clear in the target area, but when the Pathfinders

The new Pathfinder units moved to adjacent airfields within the No 3 Group area, and No 83 Sqn found itself at Wyton. Each group was supposed to supply replacement crews and support the aircraft types they had provided, but this was not always the case. By August 1942 the Pathfinder Force was suffering from a particular shortage of Lancasters, and No 83 Sqn found itself with the oldest and most well-used airframes in Bomber Command, while relying on other units' cast-offs as attrition replacements. Serviceability became so poor that the squadron was stood down on at least three occasions before the end of 1942 because it was unable to offer a worthwhile number of aircraft for operations. This particular B I (R5852) was originally used by No 207 Sqn, before being transferred to No 83 Sqn in the summer of 1942. It was in turn passed on to No 1654 HCU and finally written off on 9 September that same year when its student pilot overshot while landing at Condover (*Aerospace Publishing*)

arrived over Flensburg, they found it entirely obscured by cloud. All they could do was drop their visual target marker parachute flares on a position calculated by dead reckoning, and the first few Main Force bombers dropped on this, before the flares descended through cloud. The remainder of the bomber stream either dropped on the glow from the target, or (about a quarter) took their bombs home.

The Pathfinders led another Main Force raid on 25 August 1942, and No 83 Sqn lost two aircraft. The PFF was never large enough in its early days, and there was a particular shortage of Lancasters, since No 83 Sqn found itself with relatively old and well-used airframes. Without a means of obtaining newer replacement aircraft, and having instead to rely on other squadrons' cast-offs as attrition replacements, serviceability became so poor that the unit was stood down on at least three occasions before the end of 1942, because it was unable to offer a worthwhile number of aircraft for operations.

During the early days of the PFF, target marking was a fairly primitive art. After an initial period with no target marking devices of any sort, the Force then relied on the use of makeshift target markers, which were 250- or 4000-lb bomb cases filled with a mix of incendiary materials, including benzole, rubber and phosphorus. The smaller markers were known as 'Red Blob Fires', and the larger as 'Pink Pansies'. These burned fiercely, but were relatively easy to simulate, allowing the Germans to set off 'false markers' to distract the bombers from their targets. They entered service in September.

New markers were introduced at the beginning of 1943, which were easier to recognise and harder to imitate. These were developed in association with the pre-war fireworks industry, and entered service in mid-January 1943. The first of these was a 250-lb bomb containing 60 12-inch candles, which were ejected and ignited at a pre-set height, using a barometric fuse. These gave a 60-yard pattern on the ground in red, green or yellow.

The Pathfinders soon began to use three main types of target-marking. In perfect conditions, they employed visual ground-marking (code-named *Newhaven*). When the target was partly obscured by cloud, the ground-markers were aimed using H_2S (code-named *Parramatta*). When the ground was totally obscured, the Pathfinders used 'sky-marking', dropping parachute flares, with the Main Force bombing 'through' the flares while flying on a specified course (code-named *Wanganui*). The code-prefix *Musical* (e.g. *Musical Parramatta*) indicated that *Oboe* had been used, rather than H_2S.

Target-marking techniques developed quickly. Soon the Pathfinders did not simply mark the aiming point and leave, but instead dedicated 'backer-ups' replenished the markers, while 're-centerers' could drop flares which

Grp Capt J H Searby (centre) had taken over command of No 106 Sqn after the departure of Gibson (and his senior pilots J V Hopgood and D J Shannon) to form No 617 Sqn. If anything, No 106 Sqn's reputation was enhanced under Searby, who saw his unit's loss and early return rates remain low, while servicing figures and the percentage of aircraft offered for operations also improved, and the unit climbed the No 5 Group Bombing Ladder. Searby went on to command No 83 Sqn from May 1943, and under him, the unit's performance improved immeasurably. Searby virtually invented the role of Master Bomber, and performed this function over Turin on 7/8 August 1943 and then again during the Peenemünde raid. He is seen here with his two flight commanders, Sqn Ldrs R J Manton and R A B Smith DFC (*via Francis K Mason*)

effectively moved the aim point – often doing so to compensate for any creep-back, if Main Force bomb-aimers released short of the aim point.

For example, during the raid on Peenemünde, PFF 're-centerers' were used (under the control of the Master Bomber) to shift the aim point around the complex, ensuring the destruction of successive targets within the overall facility.

No 109 Sqn, flying *Oboe*-equipped Wellingtons, was attached to the Pathfinders from No 2 Group, but did not fly operations with the new group, concentrating instead on trials of the new guidance equipment.

Oboe worked by transmitting pulses which were received and returned by a suitably-equipped aircraft, with range being worked out by comparing the time between transmission and reception. Each aircraft used two ground stations, one transmitting a series of dots and dashes on each side of a curved track, allowing the pilot to ascertain which side of the track he was flying. The second station transmitted a 'beam' which bisected the track at the planned bomb release point, the pilot hearing a distinctive long dash at this point.

No 109 Sqn briefly operated a handful of *Oboe*-equipped Lancasters between July and October 1942, but these proved unsuitable for operations, and Wellingtons continued to form the unit's backbone until the arrival of Mosquitos in December 1942. This was because the *Oboe* system relied on the *Oboe*-equipped aircraft flying above the radar horizon (e.g. at 30,000 ft or more over the Ruhr) in order to receive and return the radar pulses from ground stations in the UK. Only the RAF's Mosquitos could fly high enough over enemy territory to receive the signals, where they were exceptionally difficult for the Germans to detect, let alone jam.

On the last night of December 1942, No 109 Sqn's new *Oboe*-equipped Mosquito B IVs acted as target markers for a 'Main Force' of eight No 83 Sqn Lancasters which bombed Düsseldorf through unbroken cloud, and yet achieved a high degree of accuracy. But *Oboe* could only be used by two aircraft simultaneously, and by only 18 per hour (six aircraft from each of three ground stations), and was no solution to the underlying need for reliable navaids for larger numbers of aircraft.

Until the arrival of H_2S, little could be done to improve target marking in cloudy conditions. The Pathfinders were accorded a high priority for H_2S deliveries, and the Stirlings of No 7 Sqn and the Halifaxes of No 35 Sqn were equipped with H_2S by January 1943.

The Pathfinder Force was re-designated as No 8 (PFF) Group on 8 January 1943, and it finally received a second Lancaster unit later that month with the conversion of No 156 Sqn from the Wellington. But January also saw the Pathfinders' best efforts occasionally being frustrated by Bomber Command planners. On 16/17 January and again the following night, the Pathfinders arrived over Berlin at their

The arrival of H_2S revolutionised Pathfinder operations. Interestingly, the group's Lancasters received the device after its Stirlings and Halifaxes. This aircraft (W4963) was used for H_2S radome airflow tests at Boscombe Down in 1942, and carried the name *"BENDALL'S FOLLY"* on the nose. This aircraft remained with the A&AEE until it was sent to the Middle East for hot weather trials in November 1944. W4963 was finally struck off charge on 11 November 1946 (*via Francis K Mason*)

appointed time, only to find the lead elements of the Main Force bomber stream already dropping their bombs. Some No 5 Group crews angrily accused the Pathfinders of tardiness, but the problem seems to have come from the planners at Group and Command.

In early 1943, the Pathfinder Lancaster crews also had to cope without the H_2S radar, which was becoming standard within other PFF units, and which was even being introduced on a handful of Main Force Lancasters. Indeed, Nos 83 and 156 Sqns still primarily operated very old B Is, and were destined to continue doing so for some time.

But the Pathfinders' stock was destined to rise significantly during the Battle of the Ruhr, when their target marking was roundly praised by Main Force crews, but where enemy fighters began to concentrate their efforts on the Pathfinders, causing heavier casualties. H_2S radar, working well in the Stirlings of No 7 Sqn and in No 35 Sqn's Halifaxes, was still unsatisfactory on No 83 Sqn's Lancasters, but the introduction of VHF radio proved to be a revelation, allowing a Master Bomber to broadcast corrections, draw attention to enemy decoy flares and prevent 'creepback'. A Master Bomber (Wg Cdr J H Searby) was used for the first time during the attack on Turin on 7/8 August 1943, and then again during the Peenemünde raid.

Another Lancaster Pathfinder unit 'arrived' in No 8 Group during April 1943 with the transfer of No 97 Sqn to Bourn from No 5 Group. This transfer was not entirely welcomed by the unit's crews, despite them receiving brand new H_2S-equipped B IIIs. Many of the personnel were fanatically loyal to No 5 Group, and felt that No 106 Sqn should have been sent in their stead. Once settled within the Pathfinders, however, the unit more than justified Bennett's choice, proving extraordinarily successful.

Things got even better during the Battle of Hamburg in July 1943, with H_2S at last working well, and with new target markers and VHF radio further enhancing bombing accuracy. The Pathfinders also had a fourth Lancaster unit, since within No 8 Group, No 7 Sqn had just traded its Stirlings for Lancasters. The following month the Canadian-manned No 405 Sqn replaced its Halifaxes with Lancasters.

Later in the year, the Pathfinders learned new lessons in the Battle of Berlin. Having become somewhat reliant on H_2S, they found Berlin to be a poor radar target, and had to relearn the art of working without it.

Perhaps the greatest tribute to the vital work of the Pathfinders can be found in the fact that in early 1942, most Bomber Command raids on targets in Germany seemed to cost the RAF more casualties than it inflicted, with hundreds of aircraft despatched, and barely a handful dropping bombs on their assigned targets. On many occasions, more aircraft were downed (each with perhaps seven highly-trained crew members) than the Germans' lost civilians, and the scale of destruction (often limited to schools, hospitals, shops and houses) was also disappointingly low. The effect on industrial production was negligible.

Without the PFF, Bomber Command's claims on resources may have been challenged more successfully by Coastal Command (and even by the medium bomber, precision-attack advocates at No 2 Group), so the Pathfinders may well have saved Harris, and his strategic bomber offensive, from ignominy and failure.

1943 – ONWARD TO BERLIN

'Bomber' Harris himself later described 1942 as marking a 'preliminary phase', during which bombing techniques were developed while he waited for new aircraft and new technology with which to prosecute the main offensive. The first few days of 1943 saw the emergence of two new bomber groups, the Pathfinder Force becoming No 8 (PFF) Group on 8 January and the Canadian units gathered within No 4 Group becoming No 6 (RCAF) Group. The latter had actually formed in October 1942, but was declared operational on New Year's Day 1943. Henceforth it would be paid for by the Canadian Government.

Apart from the extraordinary Thousand Bomber Raids, attacks by 250 aircraft had represented a 'maximum effort' during 1942. During 1943 a maximum effort would involve some 450 bombers. Moreover, from a Command dominated by the Wellington, Harris would have a force dominated by four-engined bombers, and average bombload per aircraft more than doubled.

Following an experimental *Oboe* raid on Düsseldorf by Pathfinder Mosquitos and Lancasters on 31 December/1 January, further raids were mounted using Pathfinder Mosquitos with No 5 Group Lancasters. Three of 19 Lancasters despatched against Essen on 3/4 January and two of 29 sent out against the same target on 4/5 January were lost, but accuracy was good. A follow-up raid on 7/8 January saw all 19 Lancasters return safely, but these caused less damage.

Pathfinder Mosquitos used *Oboe* to mark for 38 Lancasters which attacked Duisburg without loss on 8/9 January, and for 50 Lancasters attacking Essen the following night, suffering three losses. The *Oboe-*

Lancaster B III DV263 of No 44 Sqn displays a well-worn finish as it takes off from Waddington in late 1943. Initially coded KM-L when issued to the unit in September 1943, this aircraft was re-coded KM-M in late November. A veteran of four raids on Berlin (and damaged in action on the 27/28 November op to the German capital), DV263 was lost on its fifth trip to that most feared of targets on 20/21 January 1944 (*via Bruce Robertson*)

Members of the groundcrew confer with the pilot and crew of 'their' No 57 Sqn Lancaster after landing, eager to get to work fixing any 'snags' which may have revealed themselves during the mission. Like all bomber squadrons, No 57 had mixed crews, with *NEW ZEALAND* and *CANADA* shoulder flashes visible on the aircrew seen here (*via Bruce Robertson*)

marked offensive against Essen continued on 11/12 (with one of 72 Lancasters failing to return), 12/13 (one of 55 Lancasters being lost) and 13/14 January (when four of 66 Lancasters failed to return). Four of 79 Lancasters were lost when No 5 Group returned to Essen on 21/22 January, bombing blind through total cloud cover.

October 1942 had seen the introduction of the radial-engined Lancaster B II, a handful being issued to a flight within No 61 Sqn at Syerston. This small trials unit finally began operations on 11 January 1943.

The Hercules-powered variant had been designed in anticipation of the supply of Merlin engines being disrupted by America's entry into the war. Some expected that US industry would cease production of this 'foreign' engine in favour of indigenous powerplants, and that the pressure on Merlin production would become unbearable. In fact, the USA would dramatically increase Merlin production, making US-built Merlin engines available to a range of British built aircraft types, as well as powering the bulk of the P-51 Mustangs built.

This development made the Lancaster B II almost irrelevant before it entered service, but 1000 were ordered from Armstrong Whitworth in 1941. This order would later be cut back to only 300 aircraft when it became clear that the shortage would actually be of Hercules engines, needed for the Halifax, Stirling and Sunderland.

The Hercules-engined Lancaster climbed faster than the Merlin-powered aircraft up to 18,000 ft, and was as fast in the cruise and 'flat out'. Unfortunately, the aircraft had a lower operational ceiling.

1943 began with a major diversion from Harris's beloved strategic offensive. A 14 January directive from the War Cabinet ordered him to mount area attacks against French cities adjacent to U-boat operating bases, singling out Lorient, St Nazaire, Brest and La Pallice (in order of priority). These attacks were quite specifically not pinpoint attacks against the U-boats themselves, nor even the docks in which they were based, but aimed to devastate maintenance facilities and basic services like power, water and light, and (although this were left unstated) the locally recruited workers who augmented Kriegsmarine personnel.

Unfortunately, however, all essential services were protected by newly-built reinforced concrete U-boat pens, or dispersed into the surrounding countryside, and the offensive against Lorient and St Nazaire was destined to have little effect, except on the French civilian population. And these were exceptionally heavy attacks, with one raid on Lorient on 13/14 February marking the first time that Bomber Command dropped more than 1000 tons of bombs. Fortunately attacks against Brest and La Pallice were abandoned when the results of the raids against the initial targets became clear.

This anti-U-boat campaign began on 14/15 January, with the 122-aircraft force including six Lancasters. Target marking was accurate, but Main Force bombing was described as 'wild'. Four Lancasters were among the 157 aircraft which returned to Lorient on 15/16 January, when bombing was more effective. Lancasters played a relatively minor role in the raids against Lorient (on 23/24, 26/27 and 29/30 January, and on 4/5 February), being heavily outnumbered by other types.

However, on 7/8 February, the 323 attackers included 80 Lancasters, which contributed to a devastating attack, although three Avro bombers were lost. Lorient received an even heavier attack on 13/14 February, and 164 Lancasters outnumbered all other types in a raid which saw more than 1000 tons of bombs dropped for the first time in an unreinforced Main Force attack. Two Lancasters were lost. The final attack against Lorient came on 16/17 February, with 377 bombers being sortied. These included 131 Lancasters, one of which was lost. In eight major raids, Bomber Command dropped 4000 tons of bombs on the French port, losing 24 aircraft in the process.

On 16/17 January Bomber Command mounted its first major raid on Berlin since 1941, sending out 190 Lancasters and 11 Halifaxes. The force found Berlin ill-prepared for the attack, with half of its flak personnel away on a training course, and with inadequate air raid warnings ensuring that the streets were full. Despite cloud and haze, and consequently inaccurate bombing results, 198 people were killed on the ground (53 of them PoWs) and the *Deutschlandehalle* (Europe's biggest covered hall) was burned out after the 10,000-seat venue had been evacuated without casualties. One Lancaster failed to return.

Berlin would never be attacked so cheaply again, as was demonstrated the following night when 19 Lancasters (of 170) and three Halifaxes (of 17) were downed. One of the surviving Lancasters, flown by No 106 Sqn's CO, Guy Gibson, carried the BBC's Richard Dimbleby.

Lancasters formed the backbone of two attacks against Düsseldorf during January, with 80 aircraft (backed by three Mosquitos) attacking the city on 23/24 January, and 124 (backed by 33 Halifaxes and five Mosquitos) on 27/28 January. The second raid saw the first use of ground markers by the *Oboe* Mosquitos, backed up by PFF Lancasters. The bombing was concentrated, and caused substantial damage.

January 1943 saw the formation of a new No 1 Group Lancaster unit, No 100 Sqn, which had previously operated Vildebeest torpedo bombers in the Far East. The month also saw No 156 Sqn convert from Wellingtons to Lancasters within No 8 Group.

Period transport rolls across the bleak Syerston pan towards waiting Lancaster B II DS604 of No 61 Sqn. Car ownership was rare among Bomber Command aircrew, who were more likely to get out to their aircraft by bicycle or on a service-supplied lorry. Only the fourth B II ever built, DS604 was delivered to No 61 Sqn in September 1942. It flew no operations with the unit, and was transferred to No 115 Sqn in early 1943. Coded KO-B, it was lost on a mission to Frankfurt on 10/11 April 1943 (*via Bruce Robertson*)

Lancasters were used in two attacks against Hamburg on 30/31 January and 3/4 February. These proved relatively ineffective, despite the Pathfinders using H_2S to mark the targets. Little damage was inflicted, but the missions resulted in the loss of five of 135 Lancasters on the first night and one of 62 on the second.

In between these raids was sandwiched an attack on Köln on 2/3 February using experimental marking techniques, although both H_2S and *Oboe* proved disappointing. Three of the 116 Lancasters sent out were lost. A similar attack on the same target on 14/15 February proved no more successful. Difficulties with H_2S and sky-marking inaccuracy were responsible for bombs falling south of their aiming point in Wilhelmshaven on 11/12 February. However, in falling wide the bombs caused a huge explosion which destroyed the naval ammunition store at Mariensiel, devastating 120 acres and inflicting damage on the dockyard and town. Three of 129 Lancasters failed to return.

The campaign against Italian cities continued with an attack on Turin on 4/5 February. The 188-aircraft force included 77 Lancasters, three of which were lost. Four No 8 Group Lancasters mounted a simultaneous raid on La Spezia with 'airburst' 4000-lb blast bombs which exploded 200 ft above the ground to maximise blast effect.

On the night of 14/15 February, Sgt Ivan Hazard of No 101 Sqn flew one of 142 Lancasters from Nos 1, 5 and 8 Groups which set out to attack Milan. The aircraft was attacked over the target by a Fiat CR.42 and set on fire, igniting incendiaries that had failed to release. This in turn sent flames over the mid-upper turret and gunner, Sgt Dove, who stayed at his post to drive off the attacker even as ammunition in the turret began to explode. Despite his burned hands and face, Dove downed the fighter, which had been damaged by the rear gunner. Ignoring his wounds, and the fire burning fiercely in the fuselage, he struggled aft to assist the wounded rear gunner from his turret.

While the rest of the crew tackled the fire, Sgt Hazard managed to fly his crippled bomber home, gaining sufficient height so as to re-cross the Alps, despite losing an engine en route. Sgts Hazard, Dove, Airey (rear gunner), Bain (Flt Engineer) and Williams (navigator) were all awarded Conspicuous Gallantry Medals, while the bomb aimer, Plt Off Gates, was awarded a DSO. Two Lancasters failed to return.

Poor marking by the Pathfinders severely limited the effectiveness of a series of missions flown against Wilhelmshaven (18/19, 19/20, and 24/25 February), Bremen (21/22 February), Nuremberg (25/26 February) and Köln (26/27 February). 154 people were killed on the ground, but the RAF lost 35 bombers, including 17 Lancasters, having mounted more than 1600 sorties.

Harris's so-called 'Main Offensive' began in the Spring of 1943 with what became known as the

These Lancaster B IIs belong to the RCAF's No 408 'Goose' Sqn, based at RAF Linton-on-Ouse. The unit received its first Lancaster B IIs in late August 1943 as replacements for its Halifax B IIs, and began operations on 7/8 October. This photo was taken a fortnight later, on 21 October. The squadron discarded its last Lancaster B II in August 1944, transitioning back to Halifaxes (this time B IIIs and VIIs) (*via Bruce Robertson*)

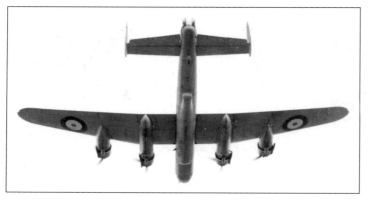

This Lancaster B II, photographed during trials with the A&AEE at Boscombe Down, shows the bulged bomb-bay doors often fitted to the variant, together with its distinctive ventral gun turret (*via Bruce Robertson*)

Air Vice Marshal The Honourable Sir Ralph Cochrane took over the exclusively Lancaster-equipped No 5 Group on 28 February 1943. Cochrane was an old colleague of Arthur Harris, and the two men saw 'eye-to-eye' on the prosecution of the bomber campaign (*via Bruce Robertson*)

Battle of the Ruhr. Harris would probably have preferred to strike against Berlin, but realised that a serious offensive against the German capital would have to wait for longer nights, improved bombing and target-marking techniques, and an answer to the menace posed by flak and fighters. This was proved (if proof were necessary) on 1/2 March, when 17 of the attacking force of 302 aircraft were lost, including seven of 156 Lancasters. Bombing accuracy was good, however, and damage was heavy. Most significantly, Bomber Command managed to knock out a Telefunken factory where a captured H_2S set (from a Stirling) was being re-assembled. The set was destroyed, but the Germans received a new one the same night from a No 35 Sqn Halifax which crashed in Holland!

The limitations of H_2S were starkly revealed during an attack on Hamburg on 3/4 March, when the Pathfinders mistook mudbanks in the Elbe 14 miles south of the city for Hamburg docks. The town of Wedel (including a naval clothing store) was hit harder than Hamburg, and ten of the 417 attacking aircraft were downed, including four of 149 Lancasters.

The Ruhr was a better target – more important to the German war economy, closer and thus more accessible to Bomber Command's bases, and with a dense concentration of important (and not merely symbolic) targets. But the cities in the Ruhr valley were not an easy target, being heavily defended by belts of searchlights, AA guns and nightfighter control boxes. The defences were so heavy, in fact, that even at the height of the battle, Bomber Command had to keep hitting other targets, from Stettin to Turin, to discourage the Germans from committing even more resources to the defence of the Ruhr cities.

The number of bombers despatched on raids increased steadily during the Battle, but began with occasional raids by as many as 600 aircraft! The first raid of the offensive was made against Essen on 5/6 March. Marking was accurate, despite a ground haze, and 442 aircraft (including 157 Lancasters) inflicted heavy damage during their 40-minute attack, killing between 457 and 482 people and destroying 3018 houses. Two-thirds of the bombs dropped were incendiaries, and of the remainder, one-third were fused for long delays. Stragglers hit six other Ruhr valley cities. Four Lancasters failed to return.

On 8/9 March, Bomber Command ranged further to attack Nuremberg with 335 aircraft. Haze prevented accurate marking, and only half of the bombs dropped hit the city. Nevertheless, damage was heavy. Two of the 170 Lancasters failed to return.

It was Munich's turn the next night, with 264 aircraft (including 142 Lancasters) attacking. Most bombs fell in the western part of the city, and 208 people were killed. Five Lancasters were lost, yet despite local flak firing 14,234 rounds and seven nightfighters being active over the target, only one RAF bomber actually fell over Munich itself.

Taking a break from the busy bomber war are the personnel of No 12 Sqn, perched on top and in front of one of the unit's Lancasters at Wickenby in 1943. The unit had replaced its Wellington IIIs with the Avro heavy bomber in November 1942 (*via Bruce Robertson*)

Lancaster B III DV238 initially served with No 619 Sqn, before going on to No 49 Sqn at Fiskerton, with whom it was photographed. Transferred to No 44 Sqn in late 1943, the bomber went missing over Berlin on 16/17 December 1943 whilst being flown by Plt Off D A Rollin and his crew. Tractors like this David Brown VIG 1/462 were typically used for towing 'bomb-trains' out to awaiting aircraft, this particular vehicle having a towing pull of 5600 lbs (*via Francis K Mason*)

A raid on Stuttgart by 314 aircraft (including 152 Lancasters) on 11/12 March was largely ineffective, but Bomber Command returned to form on 12/13 March when Essen was re-visited. 457 aircraft attacked, including 156 Lancasters, eight of which were shot down. About 200 people were killed on the ground, and Krupps was hit hard. The next major Bomber Command attack was made against St Nazaire on 22/23 March with 357 aircraft, including 189 Lancasters.

A 455-aircraft raid against Duisburg on 26/27 March was poorly marked, and resulted in little damage, but a major effort (by 396 aircraft, including 191 Lancasters) against Berlin the following night proved more successful. Three Lancasters were among the nine aircraft lost. Investigating the attack, the Gestapo assumed that local agents had flashed lights to mark the target – a stores depot at Teltow, 11 miles from the centre of Berlin, which was utterly destroyed. Luftwaffe investigators assumed this had been the work of a special unit.

The remainder of the month saw another devastating attack against St Nazaire on 28/29 March, and a return to Berlin the following night. The latter was inaccurate due to unforecast winds, and cost 21 aircraft, including 11 Lancasters. The operation against St Nazaire was the last major attack against French targets for some time, although 55 aircraft hit the city again on 2/3 April.

March had also seen the formation of three new Lancaster units, No 3 Group's No 115 Sqn converting from the Wellington, and No 5 Group gaining two brand-new units, Nos 617 and 619 Sqns.

April was a busy month for Bomber Command, with attacks against Duisburg (8/9, 9/10 and 26/27 April), Essen (3/4 April and 30 April/1 May), Mannheim (16/17 April), Stuttgart (14/15 April), Frankfurt (10/11 April), Kiel (4/5 April), La Spezia (13/14 and 18/19 April), Pilsen (16/17 April) and Stettin (20/21 April). Results varied, but marking was generally good and damage was correspondingly heavy. The initial April attack on Essen was the first occasion on which more than 200 Lancasters participated. The April raids cost 81 Lancasters in all.

When the day/medium bombing No 2 Group finally transferred from Bomber Command to the

This No 106 Sqn Lancaster limped home to a successful force-landing after being engaged by a German nightfighter over Dusseldorf on 22/23 April 1943. A veteran of numerous raids on German and Italian targets following its entry into service July 1942, R5700 was duly repaired and issued to No IX Sqn in July 1943. Coded WS-N, it was lost on a mission to Hamburg on 22/23 September 1943 (*via Bruce Robertson*)

Another nightfighter damaged B III EE140 of No 100 Sqn on 16/17 June 1943 during the raid on Cologne, causing it to force-land at the unit's Waltham base. Although this machine had only been issued to the unit on 31 May, fresh from Avro's Newton Heath factory, it was deemed too badly damaged to warrant repair (*via Francis K Mason*)

2nd Tactical Air Force in May 1943, Harris saw to it that its two Mosquito squadrons, Nos 105 and 139, were retained and transferred to No 8 Group, thus setting the stage for that organisation becoming wholly equipped with the Lancaster and Mosquito.

May followed a similar pattern to April, but with larger numbers of aircraft being despatched, and with greater participation by the growing fleet of Lancasters. The month saw major raids against Bochum (13/14 May), Dortmund (on 4/5 May, including 255 Lancasters, and 23/24 May, including 343 Lancasters), Duisburg (12/13 May, including 238 Lancasters), Düsseldorf (25/26 May, including 323 Lancasters), Essen (27/28 May, including 274 Lancasters), Wuppertal (29/30 May, including 292 Lancasters) and Pilsen (13/14 May). Some 47 Lancasters were lost during these attacks, but damage was heavy on the ground, and the first Dortmund attack saw Bomber Command inflict a record number of casualties, killing 693 on the ground (200 of these were Allied PoWs).

And although the Germans were making increasing use of decoys, the scale of destruction increased despite this. The attack against Wuppertal was particularly savage, rasing 1000 acres of the suburb of Barmen in a deadly firestorm. The best estimate of civilians killed was 3400 – five times greater than the previous record, and marking the full potential of Bomber Command's capacity for destruction and death. But even here 33 bombers were lost, giving a return of about 100 civilians per bomber, which was hardly a good exchange rate.

In the public eye, however, May's raids against Ruhr towns were over-shadowed by Operation *Chastise* (the Dams Raid), which is described more fully in Chapter Seven.

June saw the Battle of the Ruhr continuing at an accelerating pace, some 783 aircraft (including 326 Lancasters and 202 Halifaxes) attacking Düsseldorf on 11/12 June – 14 Lancasters failed to return. A total of 1292 people were killed and 140,000 were 'bombed out', and destruction was heavy. On the same night, 29 Lancasters dominated the 72-aircraft force from No 8 Group which attacked Münster in a mass trial of H_2S. Between them, the two attacks represented the biggest Bomber Command effort since the Thousand Bomber Raids.

June's attacks on Ruhr towns were generally extremely effective, especially against those towns which had not previously been attacked in strength. Casualties soared, and the final attack of the month, against Köln, killed 4377 German civilians, injured 10,000 more and bombed out 230,000.

Three more raids killed a further 1000+ Germans, including another attack on Wuppertal, which saw its eastern suburb of Elberfeld suffer the same fate as Barmen had just weeks earlier. The month's attacks saw Bochum (12/13 June), Gelsenkirchen (25/26 June), Köln (16/17 and 28/29 June), Krefeld (21/22 June), Mulheim (22/23 June), Oberhausen (14/15 June), and Wuppertal (24/25 June) all badly bombed. No less than 107 Lancasters were lost in June, with fine weather allowing the German nightfighters to gain considerable success. Losses ranged from below four per cent to a high of 8.4 per cent on the Oberhausen raid.

June also saw the low level raid against the Schneider works at Le Creusot (described in Chapter Three), and a special mission against the Zeppelin works at Friedrichshafen, on the shores of Lake Constance (Bodensee).

The latter target had been attacked on 20/21 June, 60 No 5 Group Lancasters being guided by

a Master Bomber (Wg Cdr G L Gomm of No 467 Sqn taking over from Grp Capt Slee after the latter's aircraft developed engine trouble). Due to attack at between 5000-10,000 ft, heavy flak forced the Lancasters to bomb from 15,000 ft, where they were hampered by strong winds. The factory was devastated, however, and the raiders flew on to land in North Africa. When they returned, on 23/24 June, 52 Lancasters attacked La Spezia en route.

No 426 Sqn joined No 6 RCAF Group as a Lancaster unit during June 1943, trading in its Merlin-powered Halifaxes.

The offensive continued in July, with Köln coming under heavy attack on 3/4 and 8/9 July. The first raid saw the emergence of the new *Wilde Sau* tactics, in which single-seat fighters used the light from searchlights, target markers and burning buildings to attack RAF bombers in the target area. Despite this innovation, the night's loss rate was a routine 4.6 per cent. Other Ruhr towns hit in July included Gelsenkirchen on 9/10 July and Aachen on 13/14 July. Essen received a follow-up visit on 25/26 July, and the campaign finished with an attack on Remscheid on 30/31 July. Turin was attacked on 12/13 July and the Peugeot works at Montbéliard was hit on 15/16 July.

Even as the Battle of the Ruhr continued, Harris had carefully planned his next major offensive. This was directed against Hamburg, Germany's second city, and premier port, and an excellent, distinctive

The former Zeppelin works at Friedrichshafen, on the northern German shore of Lake Constance, was used in World War 2 for making radar equipment and mines, and thus represented a vital target. Bomber Command used it to test the effectiveness of a Master Bomber, despatching 56 Lancasters (from Nos 9, 49 and 467 Sqns) and four Pathfinder aircraft on 20 June 1943. Grp Capt Slee's machine was hit by flak, and his deputy, Wg Cdr Cosme Gomm, took over as Master Bomber, transmitting corrections when the Pathfinder aircraft undershot the target with their markers. The plant suffered considerable damage, with half of the big airship shed's southern wall being blown out (*via Bruce Robertson*)

Eight aircraft participating in Operation *Bellicose* (the attack on Friedrichshafen) were damaged during their recovery at Blida and Maison Blanche, in Algeria, this No 61 Sqn machine having to be scrapped after making a heavy flapless landing (*via Francis K Mason*)

A Lancaster crew (and their groundcrew) pose with their aircraft after their return from Maison Blanche following Operation *Bellicose*. As part of Bomber Command's first shuttle mission, the Lancasters had bombed La Spezia on the return journey to Britain. Note that the gunner third from the right has returned home with a souvenir of his brief stay in North Africa – a pith helmet! (*via Bruce Robertson*)

target for H$_2$S radar, promising a high degree of accuracy in target marking. Bomber Command would drop almost 10,000 tons of bombs on Hamburg in four major raids (on 24/25, 27/28 and 29/30 July, and on 2/3 August), totalling just over 3000 sorties. The effect on Hamburg was devastating, with 1500 killed on the first night and an astonishing 40,000 on the second (most of these dying from carbon monoxide poisoning as the raging firestorm sucked the oxygen from their shelters). No fewer than 1.2 million people fled the city in the immediate aftermath of the raid, reducing the casualty figures on the last two nights.

Losses were remarkably low, totalling 1.5 per cent of the 791 attacking aircraft on the first night, 2.2 per cent of 787 on the second, 3.6 per cent on the third and 4.1 on the fourth. Bomber Command lost four of 347 Lancasters on the first raid, 11 of 353 on the second, 11 of 340 on the third and 13 of 329 on the last night. These low losses were attributed to the introduction of 'window' – strips of foil-covered paper 27 cm long and 2 cm wide which provided a blizzard of 'false returns' that effectively blinded German fighter control radar, and even the airborne *Lichtenstein* radar used by nightfighters.

'Window' had been developed months before, but its use had been embargoed to prevent the Luftwaffe finding its secret and using a similar invention against British radar. During the so-called 'Window Embargo', however, Bomber Command lost more than 2200 aircraft, a figure that might have been halved had 'Window' been used.

In the wake of the firestorm – actually caused by uncharacteristically high temperatures, low humidity and reduced rainfall over the preceding weeks, there were accusations that the RAF had set the city alight deliberately, and that Bomber Command had dropped a notably high proportion of incendiaries. In fact the reverse was true, with just under half the total tonnage comprised of incendiaries (a lower proportion than on many of the Ruhr attacks). But devastation from the bombing prevented the fire brigade from reaching the worst fires, which eventually joined together and began competing for oxygen, producing the firestorm phenomenon.

It had originally been intended that Hamburg would be bombed 'around the clock', and the USAAF's B-17s flew 252 sorties in the two days following the first RAF attack. Unfortunately, smoke from the burning city hampered their efforts, and the USAAF withdrew from the battle after two raids, although the Eighth Air Force's commander, Brig Gen Fred Anderson, flew in a Lancaster to observe the second night attack.

No 7 Sqn re-equipped with Lancasters in July, trading in its ageing Stirlings, and bringing No 8 Group closer to becoming an all-Lancaster/Mosquito force.

At this time, in advance of the planned invasion of Italy, Bomber Command received orders from the War Cabinet to undertake a brief campaign against Italian cities, with the aim of encouraging a separate Italian surrender.

An unidentified Lancaster crew board No IX Sqn's B III ED689 (WS-K) in June 1943. This aircraft was lost, along with Flt Lt J A Wakeford and his crew (Flg Off Reeves and Sgts Backler, Dohaney, Hawkridge, Owen and Wilson), during the raid on Cologne on 3/4 July 1943 (*via Bruce Robertson*)

The first raid, against Genoa, Milan and Turin by 197 Lancasters, saw Grp Capt Searby of No 83 Sqn rehearsing his role as Master Bomber for the up-coming attack against Peenemünde. The Command bombed Milan and Turin again on 12/13 August (with 327 Lancasters), and Milan alone on 14/15 August (with 140 Lancasters). It was Turin's turn again the following two nights (199 Lancasters sortied the first night). This final raid on Turin, on 16/17 August (by 154 aircraft, including 14 Pathfinder Lancasters), was destined to be the last of Bomber Command's attacks on Italian cities. These had proved pivotal in forcing the country out of the war.

Apart from the attacks on Italy, Bomber Command continued to hit German cities during August, including Mannheim (9/10 August), Leverkusen (22/23 August), Mönchengladbach (30/31 August) and Nuremberg (10/11 and 27/28 August), at a cost of 30 Lancasters.

Bomber Command's most important mission that month was mounted on 17/18 August, when 324 Lancasters, 218 Halifaxes and 54 Stirlings set out against the German rocket research establishment at Peenemünde. The attack was unique, in that the whole Main Force attempted what was a precision raid against a single target, and a Master Bomber (Grp Capt Searby of No 83 Sqn) controlled the attack, with the Pathfinders marking three aiming points in succession as the raid developed – first the scientists' accommodation block, then the rocket factory and finally the experimental facilities.

A diversionary attack on Berlin by Mosquitos drew off most of the German nightfighters, but 40 bombers (including 23 Lancasters) were lost, about a dozen of them to *Schräge-Musik*-equipped nightfighters which found the bomber stream on its way home. No 6 Group suffered 19.7 per cent losses, including two of No 426 Sqn's new Lancaster B IIs, while No 5 Group endured 14.5 per cent.

The heavy overall casualties (6.7 per cent) were deemed worthwhile, however, since Peenemünde was hit very hard, with 180 senior person-nel being killed and the V2 rocket programme put back by several months. Many bomber aircrew were decorated for their actions that night, not least Wt Off W L Wilson, a pilot with No 467 Sqn, who received a DFC, and Sgt George Oliver (his mid upper gunner), presented with a CGM. Wilson's Lancaster was hit by cannon fire after bombing Peenemünde, wounding his rear gunner and shooting away his elevator and rudder trim. Wilson evaded further attacks and flew the crippled bomber back to base, while Oliver downed the enemy aircraft and then put out the fires, with the assistance of the rest of the crew.

Two Halifax units converted to Lancasters during August 1943, No 405 Sqn with No 8 PFF Group and No 6 RCAF Group's No 408 Sqn.

Following the success of the Peenemünde raid, Harris launched a series of three attacks against Berlin, spread over a 12-night period. Mounted on 23/24 August, 31 August/1 September and 3/4 September, these raids may have been intended to mark the beginning of a full-scale onslaught on the Reich capital, but heavy losses and poor accuracy saw the full Battle of Berlin postponed.

September and October were characterised by lower casualty rates than had been seen in Hamburg and at the height of the Ruhr campaign, but this reflected the

growing efficiency of German air raid precautions and the evacuation of cities, rather than reduced bombing accuracy or effectiveness.

Following heavy losses during daylight raids, the USAAF detached the 422nd Bomb Squadron from the Eighth Air Force to fly on a series of eight Bomber Command night raids during early September. This followed the example of the Eighth's commander, Brig Gen Anderson, who had flown on two Lancaster missions against Essen and Hamburg during July. Despite impressive results and relatively low losses (two B-17s were shot down in 35 sorties), the experiment was not extended.

Main Force attacks in September and October targeted Bochum (29/30 September), Frankfurt (4/5 October), Hagen (1/2 October), Hannover (22/23, 27/28 September and 8/9, 18/19 October), Kassel (3/4, 22/23 October), Leipzig (20/21 October), Mannheim (5/6, 23/24 September), Munich (6/7 September, 2/3 October), Stuttgart (7/8 October) and the French Modane railway marshalling yards (16/17 September).

The raid against Hannover on 8/9 October was the last Main Force operation to include Wellingtons (26 aircraft). Some Vickers bombers

These photo-reconnaissance images of Peenemünde, taken before and after the 17/18 August 1943 attack on the German rocket research establiahment, clearly show how effective this raid was. The concentration of bomb craters in the post-mission photo bears testament to the accuracy achieved on this operation. It should be pointed out that although the main building in these images remains standing, and substantially intact, it has been burned out and had part of its roof blown out. Furthermore, lethal blast effects will have reduced it to a gutted shell in which nothing could have survived destruction (*via Bruce Robertson*)

would remain in service into 1944, flying diversionary raids and mine-laying operations, but the Main Force would henceforth be four-engined, apart from the Mosquito.

There was heroism aplenty during September and October 1943. During the raid on Leipzig, for example, Flt Sgt Frederick Stuart of No 426 Sqn won the CGM. His aircraft was attacked and badly damaged before reaching the target of Leverkusen (22/23 August), and was then set upon by a second fighter. Stuart's skilful flying allowed him to escape and continue on to bomb the target, before returning to base.

The following month, during one of the two raids against Hannover, Sgt Arthur Cowham, a rear gunner with No 57 Sqn, won a second CGM. On his first operational sortie, Cowham was hit in the face and his turret badly damaged, but he fought off the attacker with 'great resolution'. He refused to leave his post, despite great pain and loss of blood, and twice prevented an enemy aircraft from closing in by giving directions that meant his pilot could outmanoeuvre the fighter.

Apart from area attacks on cities, Bomber Command Lancasters also carried out a number of precision raids. No 617 Sqn despatched eight aircraft with new 12,000-lb bombs against the Dortmund Ems Canal on 14/15 September, but these were recalled due to fog in the target area. One aircraft crashed into the sea, killing the pilot (D J H Maltby, a 'Dams Raid' veteran) and his crew. The squadron launched against the same target on 15/16 September, but five aircraft failed to return, including those of another 'Dams Raid' veteran, Australian L G Knight, and the new CO, Sqn Ldr G W Holden.

This set the seal on No 617's low level bombing activities, and the unit re-trained as a high altitude unit. The following day eight No 617 Sqn Lancasters, and four No 619 Sqn machines attacked the Anthéor Viaduct but no hits were scored. One No 619 Sqn Lancaster was lost.

Two new units emerged during September, No 166 Sqn trading in its Wellingtons within No 1 Group, and No 514 Sqn forming within No 3 Group. Two more units formed in October, No 432 Sqn swapping Halifaxes for Lancasters within No 6 RCAF Group, while No 625 Sqn formed within No 1 Group.

Bomber Command operations during November and December continued to follow much the same pattern, albeit with more gaps due to poor weather, and with cloud causing a minor deterioration in marking accuracy.

The Main Force attacked Düsseldorf (3/4 November), Frankfurt (25/26 November and 20/21 December), Leipzig (3/4 December), Leverkusen (19/20 November) Ludwigshafen (17/18 and 18/19 November), Mannheim (18/19 November), Stuttgart (26/27 November), Cannes (11/12 November) and the French Modane railway marshalling yards (10/11 November).

On 3 November, Flt Lt Bill Reid of No 61 Sqn earned himself a Victoria Cross after pressing on to Dusseldorf when he would have been justified in returning to base. An initial nightfighter attack had knocked out the rear turret and wounded Reid in the head, shoulder and hands. A second attack killed the navigator and mortally wounded the wireless operator, while the mid-upper turret, elevator trim tabs, intercom and oxygen system were all knocked out. Reid's flight engineer, Sgt James

A Lancaster test-drops a 12,000-lb HC bomb (a quite different weapon to the 12,000-lb Tallboy) during mid-1943. This particular weapon consisted of three 4000-lb 'Cookies' bolted together, with the tail unit from the Capital Ship Bomb. No 617 Sqn introduced the 12,000-lb HC to service in September 1943 in an unsuccessful, and extremely costly, attack on the Dortmund-Ems Canal. The bomb was rarely used after this, and was not deemed to have been a success (*via Francis K Mason*)

No 61 Sqn's Flt Lt William 'Jock' Reid poses uneasily for the photographer, wearing a well-earned VC ribbon below his 'Wings', and fully recovered from the wounds he had suffered during the raid on Düsseldorf on 3/4 November 1943. He went on to fly with the elite No 617 Sqn. Reid survived the war and won much respect and admiration for his work on behalf of disabled Bomber Command veterans. He passed away on 28 November 2001 (*via Francis K Mason*)

Despite having endured two ferocious nightfighter attacks that had left him wounded, and with his navigator dead and two wounded gunners (one mortally), Flt Lt Reid pressed on to his target in Lancaster B II LM360 and successfully attacked Düsseldorf. He then navigated home by the stars, despite a shattered windscreen and a further nightfighter attack, and landed at the USAAF B-24 base at Shipdham, his undercarriage collapsing on landing. The aircraft is seen here the morning after (*via Francis K Mason*)

With its spinners removed to facilitate removal of the damaged airscrews and engines, Reid's Lancaster is dismantled by USAAF personnel after the crash-landing at Shipdham. Despite the damage, the aircraft was repaired and returned to service. It was subsequently written off after another forced landing at Fiskerton, in the hands of No 50 Sqn (*via Francis K Mason*)

Norris, was awarded a CGM for his efforts in assisting the wounded Reid to the target, and for then taking over and flying the aircraft back home, not mentioning his own wounds until after Reid had landed the aircraft at the USAAF base at Shipdham.

Five new Lancaster units formed during November. These were Nos 463 and No 630 Sqns within No 5 Group, and Nos 550, No 576 and 626 Sqns within No 1 Group. In December, two No 3 Group Stirling units (Nos XV and No 622 Sqns) also re-equipped with Lancasters.

The pessimistic observer might conclude that little had changed between the end of 1942 and the end of 1943. Bomber Command was still regularly experiencing loss rates in excess of the four per cent judged as being 'unsustainable' – and on some missions losses were much higher, reaching eight per cent and more. There were also occasions when little or no ordnance fell on its intended target. But this was becoming less and less common, however, with most raids achieving impressive results at relatively low cost. During the last quarter of the year, for example, there were several raids with a loss rate of below three per cent and a handful with less than two per cent losses.

The fate of far too many Lancasters was a fiery end. This aircraft broke apart and was burned out following a heavy landing at a heavy conversion unit. Wartime training was extremely abbreviated, and accidents were the inevitable consequence (*via Bruce Robertson*)

The first civil Lancaster was G-AGJI, registered to BOAC on Armistice Day 1943. Built as B I DV379, this machine was immediately allocated to BOAC, who replaced its turrets and bomb-aimer's nose-cone with streamlined fairings. A crude passenger interior was then installed, and the Lancaster was used by the airline's Developmental Flight until it was scrapped in December 1947 (*Aerospace Publishing*)

The days of Bomber Command losing more people than it killed were over, while the extent of damage to property and industry was becoming almost incredible. On several occasions during the year, Bomber Command virtually destroyed entire cities as working entities, most notably with the firestorms at Hamburg, but also at Kassel and Frankfurt. No-one should ignore the second attack on Frankfurt, during which 40,000 civilians died in a single night.

The Command had also begun what was to become its most difficult and dangerous struggle – the assault on the Reich capital, Berlin. But while Peenemünde and the 'Dams Raids' offered glimpses of success to come, there was no clear-cut victory to mark the beginning of the end, or the turning of the tide. On the Eastern Front Stalingrad had halted the German advance and turned it decisively back, while the separate Italian surrender (coming after the great victory at El Alamein the previous year) made Allied victory in the Mediterranean inevitable. But in the night skies over Germany, the bloody war of attrition continued to be desperately closely fought.

Although the Battle of Berlin began in earnest on 18/19 November 1943, and although Bomber Command mounted eight raids against the German capital during November and December (18/19, 22/23, 23/24 and 26/27 November, and 2/3, 16/17, 23/24 and 29/30 December), the battle continued into 1944, and the offensive is fully dealt with in the second Lancaster volume in this series.

The RAF's Lancaster force had more than doubled in size during 1943, with the formation or conversion of another 20 squadrons. No 1 Group was almost an all-Lancaster force, and the conversion of No 3 Group was well underway.

At the start of 1943, less than a third of the RAF's 'heavies' were Lancasters, but by the end of the year, the Lancaster outnumbered all other four-engined bombers. But the aircraft had become even more important than a 35-squadron force might suggest, since the Stirling and all Merlin-engined Halifaxes had been taken off operations against German targets before the end of the year. The Lancaster's importance would only increase during 1944-45, but that, as they say, is another story, and one which is told in Volume Two.

OPERATION *CHASTISE*

There have been times when the Lancaster's principal role – of using large numbers of aircraft to take the war to German industry, night after night – has nearly been over-shadowed by the relatively unrepresentative exploits of small numbers of aircraft operated by isolated units. In the mid-1950s, for example, the release of the film *The Dam Busters* focused much attention on just one night of the Lancaster's three-and-a-half year combat career, and it was a night which hardly typified the overall strategic bombing campaign.

The creation of a special unit for a single operation went against every fibre of Arthur Harris' being, and he normally deprecated the 'diversion' of his aircraft and units to what he often referred to as 'stunts and adventures'. After the high cost of the Augsburg raid in April 1942, and the failure of the Capital Ships Bomb three months later, Harris was more sceptical than ever of such operations, and distrustful of 'madcap inventors' who promised war-winning weapons. He was, however, won over to the idea of a 'Dams Raid' after watching trials film of a Wellington dropping an early 'bouncing bomb'.

Barnes Wallis, the Assistant Chief Designer at Vickers-Armstrong, had spent many months studying the system of dams which regulated water in the navigable rivers serving the Ruhr, and which provided drinking water, water for steel-making and some hydro-electric power. The three main dams were the Eder at Hemfurth, holding back a 202 m cubic metre reservoir, the Möhne at Gunne, restraining a 134 m cubic metre reservoir and the smaller Sorpe dam at Korbecke. No conventional bomb would be capable of destroying these massive structures (even if bombing accuracy had been sufficient to guarantee a hit), but Wallis believed that if a charge could be exploded in the water below the surface against the dam, the shock wave (constrained by the water) could compromise and eventually breach the structure.

Secret tests were conducted on a redundant dam in Wales, and these gave an idea of the amount of explosive which might be required. Wallis then designed a weapon which would skip across the water's surface, decelerating until it would sink a predetermined distance from the dam wall, exploding at a set

Surviving pilots from the 'Dams Raid' pose at Scampton in late May 1943. They are (with their decorations from the operation and 'wave' in parenthesis), front row, left to right, Flt Sgt C T Anderson (III), Plt Off G Rice (II, turned back), Flt Lt H B Martin (DSO, I), Flt Lt D J Shannon (DSO, I) and Plt Off L G Knight (DSO, I). Back row, left to right, Flt Sgt W C Townsend (CGM, III), Flt Lt J C McCarthy (DSO, II), Flt Lt H S Wilson (a 'spare'), Wg Cdr Gibson (VC, I), Flt Lt J L Munro (II, turned back), Flt Lt D J H Maltby (DSO, I) and Flt Sgt K W Brown (CGM, III) (*via Francis K Mason*)

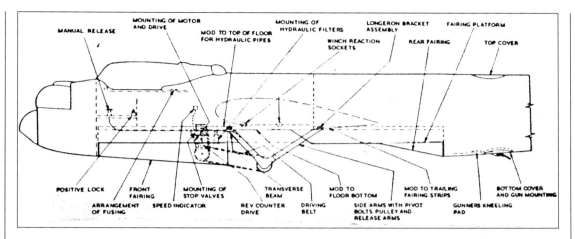

MANUAL RELEASE · MOUNTING OF MOTOR AND DRIVE · MOD TO TOP OF FLOOR FOR HYDRAULIC PIPES · MOUNTING OF HYDRAULIC FILTERS · WINCH REACTION SOCKETS · LONGERON BRACKET ASSEMBLY · REAR FAIRING · FAIRING PLATFORM · TOP COVER

POSITIVE LOCK · FRONT FAIRING · MOUNTING OF STOP VALVES · TRANSVERSE BEAM · MOD TO FLOOR BOTTOM · MOD TO TRAILING FAIRING STRIPS · BOTTOM COVER AND GUN MOUNTING · ARRANGEMENT OF FUSING · SPEED INDICATOR · REV COUNTER DRIVE · DRIVING BELT · SIDE ARMS WITH PIVOT BOLTS PULLEY AND RELEASE ARMS · GUNNERS KNEELING PAD

depth, triggered by a barometric fuse. The weapon was basically cylindrical, and was to be 'backspun' prior to release.

Wallis built and tested a number of sub-scale prototypes before approaching Bomber Command for the loan of a Lancaster – the only aircraft capable of carrying the planned full-size weapon, which weighed in at a hefty 9000-lb. Full-scale trials were authorised on 28 February 1943, and Avro was commissioned to produce a prototype of what was obliquely referred to as the Type 464 Provisioning Lancaster (ED765/G). At the same time, the decision was taken to form a new squadron, and as he completed another tour of operations (bringing his total to an astonishing 174 missions), Wg Cdr Guy Gibson was offered the opportunity to fly another 'op' by Air Vice Marshal The Honourable Ralph Cochrane, AOC-in-C of No 5 Group. Three days later Cochrane told Gibson that the mission would require a new squadron, and that he would have to form it.

Gibson hand-picked his pilots (many of whom brought their crews with them), choosing three from his No 106 Sqn and two from No 97, while the Senior Air Staff Officer of Bomber Command issued orders to all units to provide their best groundcrews. The squadron started low-level training without knowing its targets, and then flew mock attacks on the dam at Derwent Water, in the Peak District.

Wallis's bouncing bomb had to be dropped within a very tight envelope (the optimum launch parameters were 60 ft above the water and 220 mph) in order to work properly without exploding on impact or breaking up, and this required great precision in speed control and accurate height keeping over the water. The weapon also had to be dropped at an exact range from the dam. Accurate ranging was solved by using a simple wooden sight with two nails representing the dam towers, when these lined up with the real towers, the aircraft was the right distance from the dam to drop the weapon.

Accurate height-keeping was made possible through an existing device used in Coastal Command, the Spotlight Altimeter Calibrator, which used two lamps positioned to converge in a touching figure of eight pattern when the aircraft was at the selected height.

Twenty-three special Lancasters were ordered, and while these were being converted the unit trained in borrowed aircraft from the late

An official drawing of the modifications made to the *Upkeep* (Type 464 Provisioning) Lancasters. The mine spun in a clockwise direction when seen from the port side (*via Bruce Robertson*)

Two views of the 'bouncing bomb' (officially known as the *Upkeep* mine) in position under a No 617 Sqn Lancaster. The belt drive mechanism was used to spin the bomb to a pre-set speed before release, while the large fairings reduced drag and prevented turbulent airflow in the doorless bomb-bay (*via Francis K Mason*)

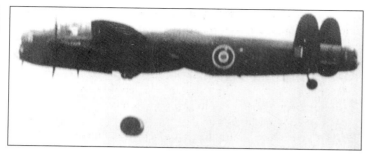

An *Upkeep* mine drops away from a 'Provisioning Lancaster' during trials at Reculver. These sorties were mostly flown by Sqn Ldr Maurice 'Shorty' Longbottom and Capt Joseph 'Mutt' Summers, both test pilots employed by Vickers. Wg Cdr Gibson and Flt Lt Martin and Hopgood also carried out trial drops at Reculver (using inert mines) on 8 May 1943 (*via Bruce Robertson*)

Seen before the application of No 617 Sqn's unit codes (AJ-T), this Provisioning Lancaster (ED825/G) was the reserve aircraft for Operation *Chastise*, and it was flown on the raid by Flt Lt Joe McCarthy RCAF when his original aircraft (ED923) went unserviceable minutes before take off. The aircraft was subsequently lost in an SOE mission on 10 December 1943. The aircraft was the third prototype Provisioning Lancaster, and was delivered to Scampton at the last moment in order to provide a replacement (20th) aircraft for one that had been damaged during training. In the event, two of the 21 available crews were prevented from participating in the raid by illness, and ED825 was used as a 'ground spare' (*via Francis K Mason*)

ED-serial range – aircraft recently delivered to squadrons were felt to be more reliable than brand new machines fresh from maintenance units. The aircraft had their dorsal turrets removed to save weight, together with the bomb doors, bomb racks and associated equipment. The bomb-bay cavity was faired fore and aft to reduce drag, and new mounting arms were added for the *Upkeep* mines, together with a motor and belt used to 'pre-spin' the weapon to a certain rpm. Despite the removal of normal bombing equipment and the mid-upper turret, the Type 464 Provisioning Lancaster was 1190 lbs heavier than a standard B I, even without the 9250-lb *Upkeep* mine.

The first successful test drop of an *Upkeep* was finally achieved at Reculver by Vickers test pilots 'Mutt' Summers and 'Shorty' Longbottom on 29 April, after a succession of failures in which early mines broke up on impact with the water. On 8 May (with 12 Provisioning Lancasters on charge with No 617) Gibson and Flt Lts Martin and Hopgood carried out drops of inert *Upkeeps* at Reculver.

Live, explosive-filled *Upkeeps* began arriving at Scampton on 13 May 1943, and were immediately loaded onto the 20 Provisioning Lancasters by then on charge. One of the latter was unserviceable, however, and was replaced by the third prototype (ED825/G) from Boscombe Down, although illness reduced the number of available crews to 19 anyway, so the new aircraft became a spare.

The decision was taken to launch the raid on the night of 16/17 May, and briefings began on the afternoon of the 15th. Each aircraft was loaded with 10,800 lbs of fuel, 18,000 rounds of tracer ammunition (12,000 in the rear turret) and a variety of incendiaries and markers, which had to be thrown out of the aircraft manually. The attack was mounted by three waves of Lancasters, consisting of nine, five and five aircraft each. The first wave was led by Gibson himself, with Flt Lt H B Martin DFC and Sqn Ldr H M Young DFC as deputies. This set off from Scampton in three groups of three at ten-minute intervals, and was tasked with attacking the Möhne Dam, with any remaining aircraft then pressing on to the Eder Dam.

The first wave came under inaccurate anti-aircraft fire over Holland, but the third section then encountered heavier opposition as it crossed the Rhine. Flt Lt W Astell's aircraft (ED864/G) was set on fire and crashed a few moments later. Meanwhile, Gibson's section were arriving at the Haarstrang Ridge – the initial point for the attack on the Möhne Dam. All had already started spinning their *Upkeeps* (a steady 500 rpm had to be reached ten minutes before dropping), and Gibson flew in low 'to take a look' while his wingmen orbited.

Each attack had to be made from the same direction, pulling up to clear a spit of land, before diving down to 60 ft, with nine seconds left to line up the aircraft and stabilise the speed. Aircraft then had to climb steeply to starboard to avoid flak defences in nearby Gunne. Gibson then made his attack (in ED932/G), but his mine detonated short of the dam. The plan called for a three-minute interval between attacks to allow the water to settle, and this gave Gibson time to reposition as Flt Lt J V Hopgood made his run. The flak was intense, and Hopgood's aircraft (ED925/G) was hit in both port engines and the starboard wing was set alight. The *Upkeep* bounced over the dam and exploded near the power station beyond it, but ED925/G was mortally damaged and crashed. Two crewmen managed to escape by parachute.

Gibson then flew in again as Martin made his attack, drawing off some of the flak and adding his gunner's fire to those of Martin (in ED909/G) to suppress the defences. Gibson positioned his aircraft just ahead of Martin's, offset slightly to starboard. Martin's *Upkeep* veered to the left and exploded against mudbanks to the left of the dam. Gibson attacked the dam from behind as Young flew in (in ED887/G), the latter's mine hitting the dam and exploding in contact. The parapet was already crumbling as Flt Lt D J H Maltby attacked (in ED906/G), this time with Gibson to port and Martin to starboard, and with all three gunners firing tracer into the flak positions. Maltby's *Upkeep* increased the size of the breach caused by Young's bomb, and Gibson's radio operator sent the codeword ('Nigger' – the name of Gibson's dog, killed in a road accident a day earlier) to No 5 Group.

Gibson ordered Martin and Maltby to return, but pressed on to the Eder Dam with Young, and the three aircraft still carrying mines.

The Eder Dam was an even tougher nut to crack. The initial approach had to be made at about 1000 ft to clear a Schloss, then after the turn onto the attack heading, the aircraft had only seven seconds to line up, stabilise and drop their weapon. The bombers then had to manoeuvre hard to avoid a hill beyond the undefended dam. Flt Lt D J Shannon RAAF made two runs, but was unable to get down to 60 ft after the diving turn, and was ordered to hold off while Sqn Lde H E Maudslay (in ED937/G) made two equally unsuccessful attempts.

Shannon then made two more runs, dropping his *Upkeep* successfully on the second of these. Maudsley then dropped his mine, which exploded on the dam without first bouncing on the water. It was officially concluded that this explosion caused Maudslay's aircraft to crash, although post-war research proved that the aircraft actually flew

The Type 464 Provisioning Lancasters were stripped of their mid-upper gun turrets to save weight, leaving only the front and rear turrets, with a single gun in a floor hatch behind the bomb-bay. This is another view of ED825/G (*via Bruce Robertson*)

Although ED817/G wore the codes AJ-C, it was not the aircraft flown by Plt Off W H T Ottley on Operation *Chastise* – he used ED910/G. Indeed, this machine did not participate in the mission, having instead been employed in the dropping trials at Reculver. The second prototype Type 464 Provisioning Lancaster, ED817/G remained in RAF service until it was Struck off Charge on 23 September 1946. Following the 'Dams Raid', the surviving Provisioning Lancasters were used for carrying outsize weapons like Grand Slam and the 12,000-lb HC bomb, and several (including the aircraft used by Gibson himself) survived the war. Regrettably, none were set aside for preservation (*via Bruce Robertson*)

133 miles along the route home (perhaps with crew casualties and damage), the pilot reporting his attack seven minutes after the explosion, and being shot down by flak about 50 minutes later.

The final first wave aircraft which still had an *Upkeep* then attacked the dam. The mine of Plt Off L G Knight RAAF punched a hole in the dam from which issued a massive horizontal jet of water, before the breach widened towards the impact point of Shannon's *Upkeep*. The aircraft then ran for home, Gibson flying via the Möhne to make a visual reconnaissance. Sqn Ldr Young had flown higher than his wingmen on the way to the target, and he and his crew were downed by coastal flak batteries as they tried to make their escape. Four of the first wave thus 'failed to return'.

The second wave of five aircraft suffered proportionally worse. While the first and third waves routed directly across the North Sea and the southern part of the low countries, the second wave routed further north, turning south to run in over the Zuider Zee before joining the same outbound route at the Rhine, downstream from Wesel. This longer route meant that the second wave actually took off before the first, and suffered its first loss at 2257 hrs, before the first loss from the first wave.

The second wave was faced with a very different task to that of the first, its target being the Sorpe Dam. This was recognised as being a more difficult target than the other two dams, since it was of very different construction, with a concrete core reinforced by concrete-capped earth banks. This in turn necessitated an entirely different type of attack, with the aircraft having to fly along the axis of the dam, dropping the weapon next to the target, ten to fifteen feet from the centre, without imparting any spin. Such a hit was not expected to breach the dam, but was expected to force the Germans to empty the reservoir in order to repair the severe leaks caused by the mines.

The second wave was to have been led by Flt Lt J C McCarthy RCAF, but his aircraft (ED923/G) went unserviceable with a hydraulic fault, and problems with the spare delayed his take off by 20 minutes, making him the last of the wave to depart. While McCarthy and his crew manned the spare, Flt Lt R N G Barlow RAAF took off (in ED927/G), but collided with overhead cables near Wesel (or may have been shot down) and crashed while attempting a forced landing. The aircraft burned out, but the mine was recovered intact by the Germans.

Next off was Flt Lt J L Munro (RNZAF), who ran into heavy flak as he crossed Vlieland (in ED921/G), losing the master compass, the hydraulics to the rear turret, the intercom and the R/T. With no effective defence against enemy aircraft, and with no means of communicating with his crew or base, Munro reluctantly turned back. The third aircraft (ED934/G) in the wave took off at 2130 hrs, flown by Plt Off V W Byers RCAF, and was hit by flak as it crossed the Dutch coast. The aircraft crashed into the sea with the loss of all on board.

Plt Off G Rice (in ED936/G) took off next, but was destined not to reach the Dutch coast. His aircraft actually hit the sea, tearing off the

Upkeep and tailwheel and sending a tidal wave of water back down the fuselage, soaking the rear gunner. With his weapon gone, Rice turned for home, and landed as the hydraulic fluid drained away.

Having finally got into the air in the spare aircraft (ED825/G), McCarthy struggled to catch up with his planned schedule, crossing the Dutch coast shortly after his unfortunate colleagues. With an inaccurate compass deviation card, McCarthy struggled to find his target, but did eventually reach it at 0015 hrs. Hindered by a tall

church spire on the approach, McCarthy made nine runs before releasing his *Upkeep*. He was unsure whether he had damaged the structure, and recce photos showed cloudy water in the compensating basin, suggesting a leak. In fact, the Sorpe had held together, and the cloudy water was caused by mud hurled over the parapet in the explosion!

McCarthy had an eventful flight home, thanks to the inaccurate compass, and at one point found himself pounding back and forth at a mere 50 ft over the heavily defended railway marshalling yards at Hamm, trying to get his bearings. He landed at Scampton at 0323 hrs.

The third wave of five aircraft was intended as a 'mobile reserve', hitting whichever targets remained after the attacks by the first and second waves. The five aircraft took off at short intervals from midnight, and followed the same outbound route as the first wave had done, making it inevitable that they would be fiercely opposed by the already alerted German defences. The crews of the last wave would also have to overcome pre-dawn mist on their way home, overflying enemy territory just as dawn was breaking.

The second aircraft (ED865/G) in the final wave, flown by Plt Off L J Burpee RCAF, was hit by flak and crashed near Gilze-Rijen airfield, while the first Lancaster (ED910/G) in the wave, flown by Plt Off W H T Ottley was downed only a little further along the route, north of

Despite his oft-expressed distaste for and opposition to what he called 'diversions', 'Bomber' Harris (standing at the extreme left) was enthusiastic about the 'Dams Raid', and made sure he was present at Scampton as the returning crews debriefed (*via Bruce Robertson*)

An unusual PR photo showing Canadian 'Dambusters', drawn from the various crews. Standing, left to right, are Sgts Oancia, Sutherland and O'Brien, and Flt Sgts Brown, Weeks, Thrasher and Deering, Sgt Radcliffe, Flt Sgt McLean, Flt Lt McCarthy and Flt Sgt McDonald. Crouching in front are Sgt Pigeon, Plt Off Taerum, Flg Off Walker, Sgt Gowrie and an unidentified pilot officer (*via Bruce Robertson*)

This collage of photographs of the breached Möhne Dam were taken by Spitfire PR XIs of No 541 Sqn. The same unit had earlier provided crucial aerial coverage of the dams for No 617 Sqn during the planning phase of the 'Dams Raid'. Indeed, No 541 Sqn had first overflown the Möhne on 25 January 1943, and regularly returned to this location in the four months leading up to the mission to provide photos that allowed a detailed model of the target to be built (*via Bruce Robertson*)

Another No 541 Sqn recce photo of the Möhne Dam following Operation *Chastise* shows water pouring through the breach caused by Sqn Ldr Young's *Upkeep*. The dam was already crumbling as Flt Lt Maltby's *Upkeep* was released, while Flt Lt Hopgood's weapon bounced over the parapet and (contrary to popular mythology) Wg Cdr Gibson's and Flt Lt Martin's mines exploded hundreds of feet short of the dam (*via Francis K Mason*)

Hamm, at 0235 hrs. Both aircraft exploded on impact, although the tail gunner in ED910/G survived when his turret was thrown clear as the bomber blew up. The explosions were seen in the third aircraft (ED918/G) in the final wave, flown by Flt Sgt K W Brown RCAF.

Brown flew past the Möhne Dam on his way to the Sorpe, and noted the massive breach in the first target. With thick mist around the Sorpe, he dropped flares before making several runs against the dam, finally releasing his mine at 0314 hrs. Brown then flew home, dropping unused incendiaries on 'targets of opportunity', and surviving vicious flak as he ran out over the Helder Peninsula at dawn.

The final Lancaster (ED914/G) to take off – at 0014 hrs – was flown by Flt Sgt C T Anderson. With gathering mist and the moon dropping lower behind the aircraft, his crew found it more and more difficult to identify landmarks and waypoints. To further complicate the task of navigation, Anderson's target was changed from the Diemel to the Sorpe, and (with his rear turret out of action) he was then forced to dog-leg around Hamm, whose defences had been 'woken up' by Ottley's ill-fated aircraft. Dispirited, uncertain of their position, and with no rear turret, and with dawn less than 90 minutes away, Anderson turned back. His actions were understood and even endorsed by many of the other survivors, but not by the squadron hierarchy, and he was destined to be posted away with almost indecent haste.

The penultimate Lancaster (ED886/G) to take off was flown by Flt Sgt W C Townsend, who was lucky to stay on track after flying through intense flak some 16 minutes after crossing the enemy coast. His luck held, although the massive floods spreading out from the shattered Möhne Dam made navigation increasingly difficult. Townsend attacked what he thought was the Ennepe Dam (but which was probably the Bever Dam), after making three dummy runs, and then obeyed orders to re-visit the Möhne Dam for a final recce. He then flew home at maximum boost and minimum altitude, ED886/G zipping along at 240-270 mph, climbing only to avoid trees, houses and power lines!

Dawn began to break while Townsend was still over Germany, and by the time he ran out between the Dutch islands of Vlieland and Texel, enemy flak gunners could see him well enough

to bounce their shells off the sea surface in their attempts to shoot him down. After 90 minutes of daylight, Townsend landed at 0615 hrs, having shut down one engine before crossing the English coast. His sortie went largely ignored in subsequent accounts of the mission, but was regarded by many pilots as having been the most courageous example of airmanship performed that night.

A German photograph of the breached Möhne Dam the day after the raid. The size of the breach caused by a single *Upkeep* (and the massive pressure of the water held back by the dam!) is remarkable. One aircraft, and four aircrew, were lost during the attack on the Möhne (*via Francis K Mason*)

The mission was held up as a great success, and was certainly an extremely valuable propaganda weapon, but its material effect has always been controversial, beyond the bare fact that 330 million tons of water were released when the two dams burst. Some 1294 people were drowned downstream from the Möhne Dam, but almost half were Russian and Ukrainian PoWs. Three power stations and five pumping plants were destroyed, and twelve more were severely damaged. Much livestock was killed, and water supplies throughout the Ruhr were disrupted for a month. Domestic electricity supplies to Bochum, Dortmund, Hagen and Hamm were also constrained.

The breaching of the Eder Dam caused fewer casualties, but heavier damage, with 25 road/rail bridges swept away, and the railway station at Gifflitz and the bridge and main line to Hamburg being destroyed too. The Fulda and Weser rivers needed dredging and bridges and banks repairing, although these took just six weeks to complete.

The repairs (and improved dam defences throughout Germany) diverted huge numbers of personnel from other duties, and some believe that the task even prevented the Germans from completing the Normandy defences before D-Day. But the vital earth dam at Sorpe remained intact, and would almost certainly have withstood the impact of all ten of the second and third waves' *Upkeeps*.

No 617 Sqn seemed at the time to have succeeded beyond all expectations, however. But even then the high cost of the mission was apparent. Of 19 Lancasters and 133 aircrew despatched, eight aircraft failed to return, with the loss of 56 aircrew, only three of whom survived. And these men were the 'cream' of Bomber Command, whose loss represented a major blow. Many still believe that they were 'thrown away' on a high-profile but ultimately wasteful mission.

And although Gibson and No 617 Sqn won great acclaim, recognition was denied to many of those who took part. Gibson was awarded the VC, and the five surviving officer pilots who had attacked the dams received DSOs, while two sergeants gained CGMs. Fourteen DFCs were promulgated, along with twelve DFMs, but six of these went to Gibson's own crew, and some crews went entirely unrecognised.

Harris professed himself to be delighted by the outcome of the raid, although its main advantage to him was that it had raised the public profile and perceived importance of his Command to the extent that he would never again be forced to sit by while the Admiralty (or anyone else) diverted squadrons to what he considered to be 'sideshows'.

APPENDICES

APPENDIX A

BOMBER COMMAND AIRCRAFT TYPES:

Operations and Losses

	Operations despatched			Losses	Ops per loss
	Bomber	Other	Total		
Lancaster	148,403	7789	156,192	3832	40.76
Halifax	73,312	9461	82,773	2232	37.08
Wellington	37,412	9997	47,409	1709	27.74
Mosquito	28,639	11,156	39,795	396	100.5
Hampden	12,893	3648	16,541	607	27.25
Blenheim	11,332	882	12,214	534	22.87
Stirling	11,074	7366	18,440	769	23.98
Whitley	8996	862	9858	431	22.87
Boston	1597	12	1609	46	34.98
Ventura	997	-	997	42	23.74
Manchester	983	286	1269	76	16.70

APPENDIX B

BOMBER COMMAND AIRCRAFT TYPES:

Operations and Bomb Tonnage

	Operations despatched		Bomb tonnage	Tons per bomber op
	Bomber	Total		
Lancaster	148,403	156,192	608,612	4.1
Halifax	73,312	82,773	224,207	3.06
Wellington	37,412	47,409	41,823	1.12
Mosquito	28,639	39,795	26,867	0.94
Hampden	12,893	16,541	9115	0.71
Blenheim	11,332	12,214	3028	0.27
Stirling	11,074	18,440	27,821	2.51
Whitley	8996	9858	9845	1.09
Boston	1597	1609	952	0.60
Ventura	997	997	726	0.72
Manchester	983	1269	1826	1.86

APPENDIX C

BOMBER COMMAND'S FRONTLINE* AIR ORDER OF BATTLE, APRIL 1943

Second-line and non-bomber units omitted

No 1 Group (HQ Bawtry, AOC AVM E A B Rice)

Breighton	No 460 Sqn	Lancaster
Elsham Wolds	No 103 Sqn	Lancaster
Grimsby	No 100 Sqn	Lancaster
Hemswell	three squadrons	Wellington
Holme	No 101 Sqn	Lancaster
Ingham	one squadron	Wellington
Kirmington	one squadron	Wellington
Wickenby	No 12 Sqn	Lancaster

No 2 Group (HQ Huntingdon)
Medium bombers only – three squadron of Venturas, three of Mitchells, two of Mosquitos and four of Bostons

No 3 Group (HQ Exning, AOC AVM R Harrison)

Bourn	one squadron	Stirling
Chedburgh	one squadron	Stirling
Downham Market	one squadron	Stirling
East Wretham	No 115 Sqn	Lancaster
Lakenheath	one squadron	Wellington/Stirling
Newmarket	one squadron	Stirling
Oakington	one squadron	Stirling
Stradishall	one squadron	Stirling

No 4 Group (HQ York, AOC AVM CR Carr)
Four squadrons of Wellingtons, four fully equipped with Halifaxes, two with a mix of Whitleys and Halifaxes and one with Whitleys only

No 5 Group (HQ Grantham, AOC AVM The Hon R Cochrane)

Bardney	No 9 Sqn	Lancaster
Bottesford	No 467 Sqn	Lancaster
Fiskerton	No 49 Sqn	Lancaster
Langar	No 207 Sqn	Lancaster
Scampton	No 57 Sqn	Lancaster
Skellingthorpe	No 50 Sqn	Lancaster
Syerston	Nos 61 and 106 Sqns	Lancaster
Waddington	No 44 Sqn	Lancaster
Woodhall Spa	No 97 Sqn	Lancaster

No 6 (RCAF) Group (HQ Allerton Park, AOC AVM G E Brookes)
Six squadrons of Wellingtons and three of Halifaxes

No 8 (PFF) Group (HQ Wyton, AOC AVM D C T Bennett)

Graveley	No 83 Sqn	Lancaster
Warboys	two units	Mosquito/ Wellington
Wyton	one squadrons	Halifax

By April 1943, Bomber Command's frontline strength was already dominated by the Lancaster, with one group (No 5) fully equipped, and another (No 1) converting. The frontline thus included 17 Lancaster squadrons, 11 with Halifaxes and seven with Stirlings, giving a total of 35 heavy bomber units (with 682 aircraft) plus 20 squadrons of light and medium bombers with a further 454 aircraft. This is misleading, however, since most of the 'medium' bombers were Wellingtons, which could carry a 4000-lb bomb as far as Berlin – a heavier load carried further than was routinely dropped by the USAAF's contemporary 'heavies'. With the introduction of the supposedly 'light' Mosquito, the RAF gained a light bomber with the same payload/range capability as the Wellington.

APPENDIX D

WARTIME LANCASTER UNITS

The following appendix gives details of Lancaster units only up to and including VE-Day. It does not include those squadrons which only used the Lancaster post-war (Nos 18, 37, 38, 40, 70, 82, 104, 120, 148, 160, 178, 179, 203, 210, 214, 224, 279, 541, 621 and 683 Sqns), nor those units which operated the Lincoln without having first operated the Lancaster (Nos 151, 192 and 199 Sqns).

No 7 SQN
No 7 Sqn traded its Stirlings for Lancasters from July 1943, as part of No 8 (PFF) Group, and remained based at Oakington, Cambs.

No IX SQN
Wellingtons were traded for Lancasters from August 1942, at Waddington, as part of No 5 Group. The unit subsequently moved to Bardney in April 1943. It mounted three attacks on the *Tirpitz*, the first in September 1944 (operating from Yagodnik, in Russia) and then in October and November, operating from Lossiemouth. Flt Sgt George Thompson was serving with No IX Sqn when he won his VC on 1 January 1945.

No 12 SQN
No 12 Sqn traded its Wellingtons for Lancasters in November 1942, remaining with No 1 Group at Wickenby for the rest of the war.

No XV SQN
No XV Sqn converted from Stirlings at Mildenhall in December 1943, remaining there with No 3 Group for the remainder of the war. From Autumn 1944, No XV began precision radar bombing through cloud, using G-H equipment.

No 35 ('MADRAS PRESIDENCY') SQN
No 35 Sqn had joined No 8 (PFF) Group as a Halifax unit, but traded these for Lancasters in March 1944.

No 44 ('RHODESIA') SQN
Within No 5 Group, No 44 Sqn became the RAF's first Lancaster unit, commencing its conversion from the Hampden in December 1941. The unit gained the 'Rhodesia' name in September 1941 in recognition of that colony's outstanding contribution to the war effort. The unit received increasing numbers of Rhodesian personnel, and there was an interchange of crews between Nos 44 and 97 Sqns in order to bring as many of Bomber Command's Rhodesians into the new 'Rhodesia Squadron'. It was recognised, however, that No 44 would never be 'Rhodesian' in the sense that the Article XV units were Australian, Canadian or New Zealand. The unit participated in the raid against the MAN Diesel factory at Augsburg, and in April 1942 detached to Lossiemouth for operations against *Tirpitz*. The unit was based at Waddington, moving to Dunholme Lodge in May 1943, and to Spilsby in September 1944.

No 49 SQN
A leading No 5 Group unit, No 49 converted from Manchesters to Lancasters at Scampton in June 1942. The unit moved to Fiskerton in January 1943, to Fulbeck in October 1944 and to Syerston in April 1945. It led the No 5 Group dusk attack against Le Creusot in October 1942, and participated in many high-profile attacks.

No 50 SQN
No 50 Sqn converted from the Manchester in May 1942 at Skellingthorpe as part of No 5 Group. The unit was briefly based at Swinderby between June and October 1942, before returning to Skellingthorpe.

No 57 SQN
The Wellingtons of No 57 Sqn were transferred to No 5 Group to compensate for the transfer of No 83 Sqn to the newly-formed Pathfinder Force. The unit's Wellingtons were then replaced by Lancasters from September 1942 at Scampton. No 57 Sqn moved to East Kirkby in August 1943.

No 61 SQN
No 5 Group's No 61 Sqn traded Manchesters for Lancasters at Syerston in April 1942. The unit became the first to operate the Hercules radial engined B II in January 1943, but was never fully equipped. Briefly loaned to Coastal Command for ASW sweeps in the Bay of Biscay, No 61 Sqn briefly operated from St Eval, but moved permanently to Skellingthorpe in November

1943, albeit with a brief sojourn at Coningsby between February and April 1944.

No 75 ('NEW ZEALAND') SQN
Within No 3 Group, No 75 Sqn traded its Stirlings for Lancasters in March 1944 at Mepal. The unit played a major part in the minelaying campaign and in the offensive against German oil production.

No 83 SQN
No 83 Sqn traded in its Manchesters for Lancasters in May 1942 at Scampton. On 15 August 1942, No 83 Sqn was No 5 Group's contribution when each Bomber Command Group was asked to donate a unit to form the new No 8 (PFF) Group, moving to the former No 3 Group airfield at Wyton. The squadron was transferred back to continue Pathfinder operations within No 5 Group in April 1944, moving to Coningsby, where it remained.

No 90 SQN
The Lancaster was No 90 Sqn's third four-engined heavy bomber type of the war, having previously operated Fortresses and Stirlings with No 3 Group. It began re-equipping with Lancasters in May 1944 at Tuddenham.

No 97 ('STRAITS SETTLEMENTS') SQN
No 97 Sqn became the RAF's (and No 5 Group's) second Lancaster unit when it replaced its Manchesters at Coningsby from January 1942. The squadron moved to Woodhall Spa in March. After participating in the low-level Augsburg raid, the unit transferred to No 8 (PFF) Group and Bourn in April 1943, in time for the Battle of the Ruhr. It returned to No 5 Group and Coningsby in April 1944.

No 100 SQN
No 100 Sqn was a latecomer to Bomber Command, despite having been one of the most successful night bomber units of the World War 1. The unit had transitioned to the torpedo bomber role in 1933, and began the war in the Far East, where it was virtually destroyed. The unit reformed within No 1 Group in December 1942, and began receiving Lancasters at Waltham (Grimsby) in January 1943. The unit moved to Elsham Wolds in April 1945.

No 101 SQN
Part of No 1 Group, No 101 Sqn converted from Wellingtons to Lancasters from October 1942 at Holme-on-Spalding Moor. The unit moved to Ludford Magna in June 1943, and after the Peenemünde raid of 7/8 October 1943, it began using ABC jamming equipment operationally, and continued to mount bombing and jamming raids until the end of the war.

No 103 SQN
No 103 Sqn was another No 1 Group unit, trading its Halifaxes for Lancasters at Elsham Wolds from October 1942. One of the unit's aircraft, ED888, completed an astonishing 140 ops, but was not selected for preservation.

No 106 SQN
The Manchesters of No 106 Sqn (a No 5 Group unit at Coningsby, commanded by Wg Cdr Guy Gibson) gave way to Lancasters in May 1942. The unit moved to Syerston in September 1942, and to Metheringham in November 1943. Sgt Norman Cyril Jackson was serving with No 106 Sqn when he won his VC during a raid on Schweinfurt on 26/27 April 1944.

No 115 SQN
No 115 Sqn was the first unit in No 3 Group to convert to the Lancaster, transitioning from the Wellington during March 1943 at East Wretham. The unit moved to Little Snoring in August 1943, and to Witchford in November 1943. Between March 1943 and May 1944, No 115 Sqn operated the B II. The unit generally used the code letters KO. Its C Flight (which used the codes A4) split off in October 1944 to form the nucleus of No 195 Sqn. A new C Flight then formed, (using the codes IL), and this disbanded in August 1945.

No 138 SQN
Best known for its SOE support role, No 138 Sqn joined Bomber Command's No 3 Group at Tuddenham in March 1945, and its new Lancasters (wearing AC codes) flew 105 sorties on nine missions before the end of the war.

No 149 ('EAST INDIA') SQN
No 149 Sqn was one of the No 3 Group Stirling squadrons that converted to Lancasters during 1944.

The unit received its first Lancasters at Methwold in August 1944. These used the unit codes OJ.

No 150 SQN

After nearly two years in North Africa and Italy, No 150 Sqn reformed in No 1 Group as a Lancaster unit at Hemswell in November 1944. It used IQ codes, and flew 827 sorties before the end of the war.

No 153 SQN

Another former Desert Air Force unit, No 153 Sqn reformed within No 1 Group in October 1944 at Kirmington. The unit and its P4-coded Lancasters moved to Scampton later the same month.

No 156 SQN

No 156 Sqn (then equipped with Wellingtons) had been No 3 Group's contribution to the new No 8 (PFF) Group when it formed. It converted to GT-coded Lancasters at Warboys in January 1943, moving to Upwood in March 1944.

No 166 SQN

GB-coded Wellingtons gave way to Lancasters with No 1 Group's No 166 Sqn at Kirmington in September 1943.

No 170 SQN

In October 1944, No 170 Sqn reformed at Kelstern (from C Flight, No 625 Sqn) as a No 1 Group Lancaster unit. Its TC-coded aircraft then moved to Dunholme Lodge, and in November moved again to Hemswell.

No 186 SQN

No 186 Sqn formed as a No 3 Group Lancaster Sqn at Tuddenham in October 1944, around a nucleus from C Flt No 90 Sqn. The unit's Lancasters replaced their AP-codes with XY- code letters, and moved to Stradishall in December 1944.

No 189 SQN

The unit formed on 15 October 1944 as a No 5 Group Lancaster squadron at Bardney. Its CA-coded aircraft subsequently moved to Fulbeck in November 1944.

No 195 SQN

No 195 Sqn re-formed at Witchford in October 1944 as a No 3 Group Lancaster unit, with a substantial nucleus from No 115 Sqn's C Flight. The new unit's A and B Flights (with A4-coded aircraft) moved to Wratting Common in November, joining a new C Flight which had formed there that same month with JE-coded aircraft.

No 207 SQN

No 207 Sqn traded its unreliable EM-coded Manchesters for similarly marked Lancasters in March 1942 at Bottesford. The No 5 Group squadron moved to Langar in September 1942, and then to Spilsby in October 1943.

No 218 ('GOLD COAST') SQN

Part of No 3 Group, No 218 Sqn traded Stirlings for Lancasters (wearing HA codes, with C Flight's aircraft coded XH) at Methwold in August 1944. The unit moved to Chedburgh in December 1944.

No 227 SQN

No 227 Sqn re-formed on 7 October 1944 as a No 5 Group Lancaster unit. Its aircraft wore 9J-codes. A Flight was initially attached to No IX Sqn at Bardney, and B Flight to No 619 Sqn at Strubby, before moving to Balderton later that month and to Strubby in April 1945.

No 300 ('MASOVIAN POLISH') SQN

No 1 Group's longest-serving Polish bomber unit, No 300 Sqn traded its Wellingtons for BH-coded Lancasters at Faldingworth in April 1944.

No 405 ('VANCOUVER') SQN, RCAF

Already part of No 8 (PFF) Group, No 405 Sqn traded LQ-coded Halifaxes for similarly decorated Lancasters from August 1943 at Gransden Lodge.

No 408 ('GOOSE') SQN, RCAF

No 408 Sqn actually traded Merlin-engined Halifaxes for radial-engined Lancaster B IIs at Linton-on-Ouse in August 1943. Unusually, the No 6 (RCAF) Group unit replaced its EQ-coded Lancasters with radial-engined Halifaxes in August 1944.

No 419 ('MOOSE') SQN, RCAF

At No 6 (RCAF) Group's airfield at Middleton St George,

No 419 Sqn traded Halifaxes for VR-coded Lancasters in early 1944.

No 420 ('SNOWY OWL') SQN, RCAF
Like many No 6 (RCAF) Group units, No 420 Sqn was converting to the Lancaster at Tholthorpe as the war ended. It did not fly operations with the aircraft.

No 424 ('TIGER') SQN, RCAF
No 424 Sqn was one of the No 6 (RCAF) Group units which flew a significant number of ops with the Lancasters it started receiving in January 1945 at Skipton-on-Swale. From its first Lancaster op on 1 February, the unit dropped 7200 tons of bombs!

No 425 ('ALOUETTE') SQN, RCAF
Like No 420 Sqn, the 'Alouettes' were converting to the Lancaster at Tholthorpe as the war ended. The unit did not fly operations with the Lancaster.

No 426 ('THUNDERBIRD') SQN, RCAF
The Thunderbirds followed much the same pattern as No 408 Sqn, trading Merlin-engined Halifaxes for radial-engined Lancaster B IIs at Linton-on-Ouse in June 1943. The unit replaced its OW-coded Lancasters with radial-engined Halifaxes in April 1944.

No 427 ('LION') SQN, RCAF
Although it did not receive its first ZL-coded Lancasters until early March 1945, No 427 Sqn in No 6 (RCAF) Group flew its first Lancaster op from Leeming on the 11th of that same month.

No 428 ('GHOST') SQN, RCAF
No 428 Sqn was the first of the main batch of No 6 (RCAF) Group Halifax Sqns to convert to Lancasters, although three No 6 (RCAF) Group units had previously operated Lancaster B IIs, and two (Nos 405 and 419 Sqns) had converted to B Is and IIIs the previous year and at the start of 1944. No 428 Sqn gained NA-coded Lancasters at Middleton St George in June 1944.

No 429 ('BISON') SQN, RCAF
No 429 Sqn did not receive its first AL-coded Lancasters at the No 6 (RCAF) Group airfield at Leeming until March 1945, but used these on several missions.

No 431 ('IROQUOIS') SQN, RCAF
No 431 Sqn was the second of the main batch of No 6 (RCAF) Group Halifax units to convert to Lancasters, following No 428 Sqn. No 431 received its SE-coded Lancasters at Croft in October 1944.

No 432 ('LEASIDE') SQN, RCAF
No 432 Sqn followed a similar pattern to Nos 408 and 426 Sqns, trading Merlin-engined Halifaxes for radial-engined Lancaster B IIs at East Moor in October 1943. The unit replaced its QO-coded Lancasters with radial-engined Halifaxes in February 1944.

No 433 ('PORCUPINE') SQN, RCAF
No 6 (RCAF) Group's No 433 Sqn received its first BM-coded Lancasters in January 1945 at Skipton-on-Swale, and began operations on 1 February.

No 434 ('BLUENOSE') SQN, RCAF
No 434 Sqn was the third of the main batch of No 6 (RCAF) Group Halifax units to convert to Lancasters, following Nos 428 and 431 Sqns. No 434 Sqn gained IP-coded Lancasters at Croft in December 1944.

No 460 SQN, RAAF
While still the only Australian unit in No 1 Group, No 460 Sqn began to re-equip with Lancasters in October 1942 at Breighton, having initially started to replace its Wellingtons with Halifaxes. The unit moved to Binbrook in May 1943. Its Lancasters wore AR codes.

No 463 SQN, RAAF
No 463 Sqn formed as a No 5 Group Lancaster unit at Waddington in November 1943 from C Flight of No 467 Sqn. Its aircraft wore PO and later JO codes.

No 467 SQN, RAAF
No 467 Sqn formed as a No 5 Group Lancaster unit at Scampton in November 1942. Its B Is and IIIs wore PO codes. The unit moved to Bottesford later that month, and to Waddington one year later.

No 514 SQN
No 514 Sqn formed within No 3 Group as a Lancaster bomber unit, receiving JI-coded Lancaster B IIs at Foulsham in September 1943. After a move to Waterbeach in November 1943, a third C Flight formed

with A2-coded aircraft. Merlin-engined Lancasters arrived in June 1944.

No 550 SQN
No 550 Sqn formed as a No 1 Group Lancaster unit at Waltham in November 1943, its BQ-coded aircraft moving to North Killingholme in January 1945.

No 576 SQN
No 576 Sqn formed at Elsham Wolds in late November 1943 as a No 1 Group Lancaster unit. It was formed from a nucleus provided by C Flight No 103 Sqn, and applied UL codes to its aircraft. The unit moved to Fiskerton in October 1944.

No 582 SQN
No 582 Sqn formed within No 8 (PFF) Group from elements of Nos 7 and 156 Sqns. The new unit, with 60-coded Lancasters, formed at Little Staughton in April 1944. South African Capt Edwin Swales was serving with the unit when he won his VC on 24 April 1945.

No 617 SQN
No 617 Sqn was unique in being formed to carry out a single specific operation. Assigned to No 5 Group, the new No 617 Sqn drew its crews from other Bomber Command units, and received AJ-coded Lancasters at Scampton in March 1943. Following the 'Dams Raid' in May 1943, the unit was retained for other specialised and precision attacks, moving to Coningsby in August 1943, and to Woodhall Spa in January 1944. The unit mounted a number of detachments during operations against the *Tirpitz* – to Yagodnik in northern Russia in September 1944 and to Lossiemouth in October and November that same year.

No 619 SQN
No 619 Sqn formed at Woodhall Spa in April 1943 as a No 5 Group Lancaster unit, forming around three ex-No 97 Sqn crews that had been left behind when the rest of the squadron had transferred to the Pathfinders. Its PG-coded aircraft moved to Coningsby in January 1944, to Dunholme Lodge in April and to Strubby in September.

No 622 SQN
No 3 Group's No 622 Sqn traded Stirlings for GI-coded

Lancasters at Mildenhall in December 1943, remaining under the command of Wg Cdr I C K Swales DFC, DFM.

No 625 SQN
No 625 Sqn formed at Kelstern in October 1943 as a No 1 Group Lancaster unit, forming from a nucleus provided by C Flight, No 100 Sqn. Its CF-coded aircraft moved to Scampton in April 1945.

No 626 SQN
No 626 Sqn of No 1 Group formed with UM-coded Lancasters at Wickenby in November 1943, and remained there for the rest of the war.

No 630 SQN
No 630 Sqn formed at East Kirkby in November 1943 as a No 5 Group Lancaster unit. Its LE-coded aircraft remained there for the duration of the war.

No 635 SQN
No 635 Sqn formed as a No 8 (PFF) Group Lancaster unit at Downham Market in March 1944 from B Flight of No 35 Sqn and C Flight of No 97 Sqn. The new unit, with F2-coded Lancasters, later performed operational trials of the high altitude B VI during July-August 1944, and one of its pilots, Sqn Ldr I W Bazalgette, won a posthumous VC for his actions on 4 August 1944.

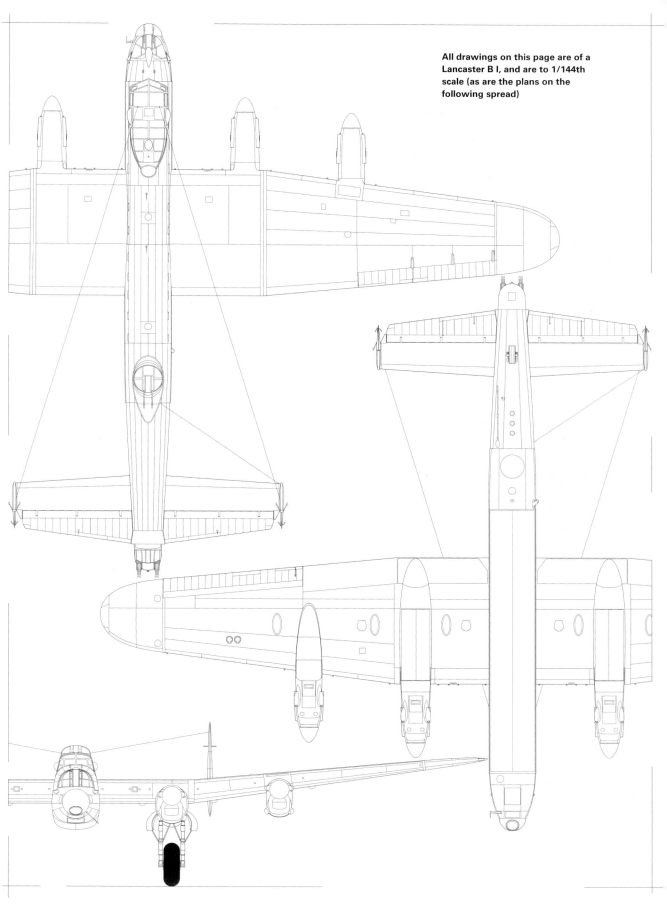

All drawings on this page are of a Lancaster B I, and are to 1/144th scale (as are the plans on the following spread)

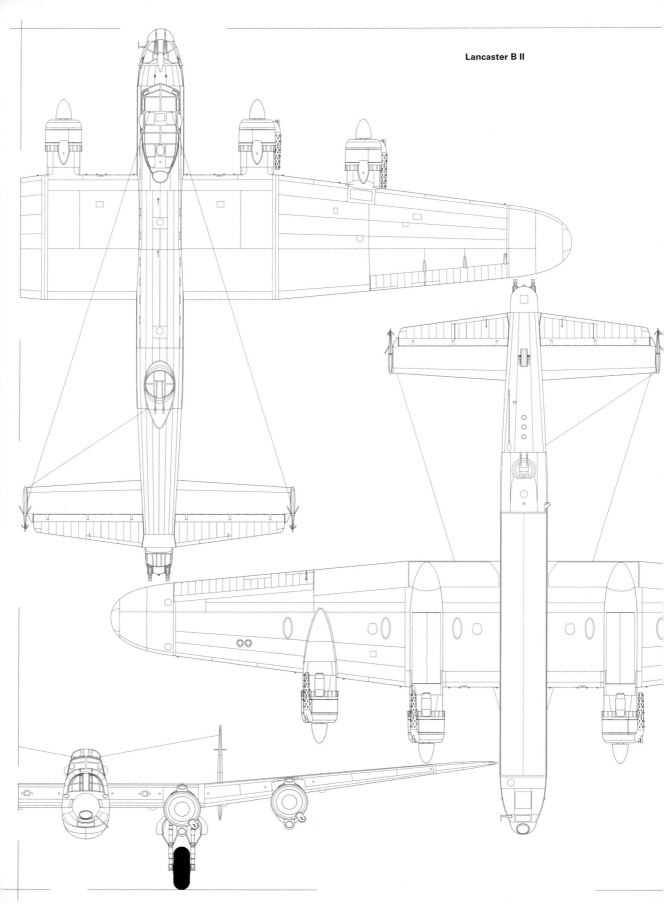

Lancaster B II

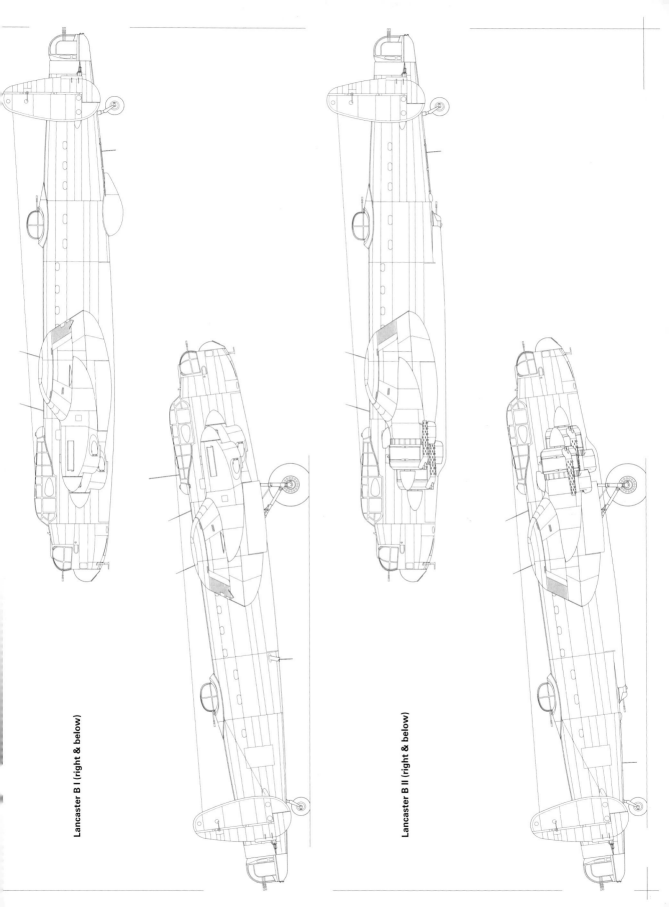

Lancaster B I (right & below)

Lancaster B II (right & below)

COLOUR PLATES

Artist's Notes

By the time the Lancaster entered service, Bomber Command colour schemes had been largely standardised, and the different demarcations between upper and lower surface colours seen on the Manchester and early Halifax were not seen on Lancasters. All aircraft were delivered with dark earth and dark green topsides, extending one third of the way down the fuselage sides, with a straight hard demarcation above the wing root. The original medium sea grey codes were soon replaced by dull (roundel) red codes, while 42-in Type A1 roundels on the fuselage were changed to the 60-in Type C1. Serial numbers were usually dull red, applied well forward of the tailplane leading edge, and were sometimes edged in yellow. Code presentation did differ from squadron to squadron, but individuality was unusual, especially in the early days of the war. Inevitably, post-war artists have tended to portray non-standard aircraft, and aircraft with nose art, but this was never common.

1

Lancaster B III EE129/MG-Y of No 7 Sqn, No 8 (PFF) Group, Oakington, Autumn 1943

This No 7 Sqn Lancaster was captained by Flg Off Tony Davies, and featured a bomb-carrying stork badge on its nose. Previously equipped with Stirlings, No 7 Sqn had been the RAF's first four-engined bomber unit, and was donated by No 3 Group as its contribution to forming the basis of the Pathfinder Force. Converting to the Lancaster in May 1943, No 7 Sqn participated in the raid on Peenemünde in August. EE129 was posted missing on the 1/2 January 1944 raid on Berlin, the aircraft being captained by Flt Lt L C Kingsbury – it had completed 311 flying hours by the time of its demise. Of the 421 Lancasters despatched on this operation, 28 were lost.

2

Lancaster B III ED480/WS-U of No IX Sqn, Waddington, February 1943

Captained by Flt Lt Bill Meyer, No IX Sqn's UNCLE was decorated with a pawnbroker's sign. This unit rapidly gained a formidable reputation with the Lancaster, and built up a great rivalry with No 617 Sqn. To this day, the two units 'bicker' as to which actually sank the *Tirpitz*, and a prized bulkhead from the ship has been stolen and re-taken many times! Having completed 250 flying hours since joining No IX Sqn fresh from the factory in January 1943, ED480 was posted missing on the 9/10 July 1943 raid on Gelsenkirchen. Of the 218 Lancasters sortied (out of an overall Bomber Command force of 418 aircraft), five did not return.

3

Lancaster B III JA852/WS-L of No IX Sqn, Bardney, July 1943

'The Lady in Red' on the nose of JA852 was augmented by the legend *Allez Haut d'Escaliers*, as well as a bizarre collection of mission marks, including an ice cream (for a mission to Turin) and a square containing an ice cream, a palm tree an RAF Eagle and the letters OHMS. The latter marked a bombing mission against Genoa, during which an engine was lost, forcing the aircraft to land in North Africa, and after which the bomber was used to transport a VIP from North Africa to Gibraltar. The aircraft was skippered on both these missions by Flt Lt Dickie Bunker, but it was lost on the 23/24 September 1943 raid on Mannheim whilst being flown by Sgt R C Ord. Delivered to No IX Sqn in the summer of 1943, JA852 had flown just 81 hours by the time it was shot down. Of the 628 aircraft that participated in this operation, 312 were Lancasters, and JA852 was one of eighteen Avro bombers to be lost.

4

Lancaster B I W4366/R-PH of No 12 Sqn, Wickenby, March 1943

The Lancasters of No 12 Sqn were unusual in having all three code letters displayed aft of the fuselage roundel. This necessitated moving the serial number from its usual location on the rear fuselage side to a position just above the tailplane. This aircraft was often flown by Sqn Ldr F B Slade, OC A Flight. Having completed 237 flying hours, W4366 was lost attacking Bochum on the night of 13/14 May 1943. It was the only loss inflicted on the 98-strong Lancaster force despatched, although 23 other Bomber Command types failed to return.

5

Lancaster B I R5508/KM-B of No 44 Sqn, Waddington, 17 April 1942

R5508 was used by Sqn Ldr John Nettleton, who won a Victoria Cross on the epic raid against the Maschinenfabrik Augsburg-Nürnberg (MAN) Aktiengesellschaft, a crucial diesel engine factory at Augsburg. For this raid, the Lancasters of No 44 Sqn wore unusual light grey code letters (with the individual aircraft letter smaller than the squadron code prefix) and were equipped with underfuselage ventral gun turrets. Despite this defensive firepower, five of the 12 Lancasters (six each from Nos 44 and 97 Sqns) were shot down, and R5508 was the only No 44 Sqn survivor. This machine was later transferred to No 97 Sqn's conversion flight, before serving time with No 1660 Heavy Conversion Unit (HCU) and No XV Sqn. R5508 was finally Struck off Charge on 15 January 1947.

6

Lancaster B I R5540/KM-O of No 44 Sqn's conversion flight, Waddington, 29 September 1942

No 44 Sqn's Lancasters had their grey codes over-painted in dull red during June 1942, reducing their conspicuity at night. R5540 was an early-build aircraft, and had the original fuselage windows but had lost its ventral gun turret. The bar painted above the letter O denoted that R5540 was the second aircraft coded 'Orange' in the unit, and that it was assigned to the conversion flight – it was occasionally flown by Sqn Ldr Pat Burnett, OC B Flight. Burnett led No 44 Sqn's nine Lancasters on the Le Creusot raid on 17 October 1942. Having initially served with No 61 Sqn (with whom it appears to have flown no operational sorties), R5540 left No 44 Sqn's conversion flight to join No 1661 HCU in late 1942. It was still serving with this unit when it crashed on landing at its new Winthorpe base on 18 January 1943 and was written off.

7
Lancaster B I W4110/KM-K of No 44 Sqn, Waddington, March 1943
W4110 was looking decidedly weary by March 1943, having joined No 44 in August 1942, and having flown 45 ops, seven of them over the Alps to Italy (shown on the bomb log by ice cream cones). The normal mount of Sgt Baldwin, the ageing Lancaster was finally lost on 13/14 May 1943 (the same night as W3466 – profile four) during a raid on Pilsen in the hands of another crew. Some 156 Lancasters and 12 Halifaxes were despatched on this raid, and nine aircraft lost. By this time W4110 had flown an impressive 524 hours.

8
Lancaster B III ED702/EA-D of No 49 Sqn, Fiskerton, March 1943
After a run of losses, an early CO of No 49 Sqn banned the application of bomb logs or nose-art on the unit's Lancasters, and this ban was strictly enforced by successive COs. ED702 was claimed by the CO, Wg Cdr Slee, soon after it was delivered, and was handed over to his successor, Wg Cdr Peter Johnson. Slee had led the Le Creusot raid on 17 October 1942, to which No 49 Sqn had contributed ten Lancasters, together with ten from No IX, nine fron No 44, twelve from No 50, ten from No 57, seven from No 61, nine from No 97, twelve from No 106 and fifteen from No 207. The aircraft flew on the Peenemünde raid on 17/18 August 1943, and was eventually lost on its 34th op, on 23/24 September 1943, over Mannheim (the same raid that JA852 – profile three – was lost). ED702 was being flown by Plt Off C F Anderson at the time.

9
Lancaster B I R5702/VN-S of No 50 Sqn, Swinderby, October 1942
Badly shot up during a raid on Hamburg on 9/10 November 1942, R5702 *Taipo* bellied in at Bradwell Bay with the wireless operator dead and the navigator injured. Remarkably, the aircraft was rebuilt and returned to service, flying with Nos 460, 100 and 625 Sqns, before finally being lost over Berlin on 15/16 February 1944. R5702 was captained

by Sgt W Ashurst on its final sortie, this particular operation seeing the largest Bomber Command force ever sent to Berlin – 891 aircraft – and the largest non-thousand bomber force sent to any target. It was also the first time that more than 500 Lancasters had been despatched, and of the 561 Avro bombers sortied, 26 were lost. Despite R5702's age (it had been delivered to the RAF in mid 1942), the bomber had spent many months being rebuilt, hence it had only flown a mere 147 hours by the time it was lost.

10
Lancaster B III ED828/VN-S of No 50 Sqn, Skellingthorpe, Spring 1943
Sqn Ldr Peter Birch's annoying habit of constantly whistling and humming 'The Donkey Serenade' infuriated his crew enough to decorate their aircraft (VN-S 'Sammy') with a braying, farting donkey – Birch was a Flight Commander on the unit. ED828 was lost on the 12/13 June 1943 raid on Bochum, 14 Lancasters out of a force of 323 Avro bombers failing to return. The aircraft had flown just 117 hours, having been delivered to No 50 Sqn in April 1943.

11
Lancaster B III ED989/DX-F of No 57 Sqn, Scampton, 27 May 1943
The CO of No 57 Sqn, Wg Cdr Campbell 'Freddie' Hopcroft, decorated his aircraft with a caricature of himself, with the head drawn in 'Plt Off Prune' style, and with a matchstick-man style body and halo. The aircraft was handed on to his successor, Wg Cdr Haskell, who was lost in it on 17/18 August 1943 during the Peenemünde raid. Bomber Command sortied 596 aircraft for this special raid on the German rocket research establishment, and 40 bombers were lost (23 Lancasters from a force of 324). ED989 had flown 119 hours by the time it was shot down.

12
Lancaster B II DS604/QR-W of No 61 Sqn, Syerston, January 1943
No 61 Sqn was the first unit to use the radial-engined B II operationally, with one flight acting as the service trials unit, although it never fully re-equipped with the type. One of DS604's sisters flew the type's first op on 11 January 1943. This early B II had the original large air cooler intakes above the engine cowlings, but lacked the airscrew spinners, lengthened B III-style bomb-aimers' nosecone, bulged bomb bay doors and ventral turret usually associated with the variant. DS604 was posted missing on a raid to Frankfurt on 10/11 April 1943, by which time it was flying as KO-B with No 115 Sqn. Of the 136 Lancasters (part of a force of 502 aircraft) sortied, five were lost. Only the fourth production B II built, and one of the first radial-engined Lancasters to be lost on operations, DS604 had flown just 49 hours since its manufacture by Armstrong Whitworth Aircraft Ltd at Whitley, in Coventry, in late 1942.

13
Lancaster B III LM360/QR-O of No 61 Sqn, Skellingthorpe, 3/4 November 1943

LM360 was flown by Flt Lt William Reid on the mission for which he was awarded a Victoria Cross. Bill Reid won a 'classic' Bomber Command VC, being awarded the ultimate military decoration for pressing on to his target despite severe damage to his aircraft and major injuries to himself. LM360's undercarriage collapsed on landing, but the aircraft was repaired and went on to serve with Nos 50 and IX Sqns. It was finally written off whilst assigned to the latter unit when it suffered a landing accident at Fiskerton on 11 November 1944.

14
Lancaster B I R5669/OL-E of No 83 Sqn, Scampton, Summer 1942

No 83 Sqn was the first Lancaster unit within No 8 (Pathfinder Force) Group, being donated to the new formation by No 5 Group. This aircraft is pictured while still based at Scampton, before the move to Wyton and the Pathfinders. This early aircraft had the original window configuration and no fairing around the mid-upper gun turret. Transferred to No 44 Sqn in the autumn of 1943, R5669 (coded KM-Z) was lost on a raid on Berlin on 23/24 December that same year. Being flown on this occasion by Plt Off T H Knight, R5669 was one of 16 Lancasters downed out of a force of 364 Avro bombers sortied.

15
Lancaster B I L7571/OF-X of No 97 Sqn, Woodhall Spa, March 1942

No 97 Sqn was the second RAF Lancaster unit, and L7571 was one of its first aircraft. The bomber is seen here with A-type roundels and fin-flashes, and the light grey codes used before May-June 1942. It has an unfaired mid-upper turret and no ventral armament. No 97 Sqn later transferred to the Pathfinders, gaining brand-new H_2S-equipped B IIIs in the process. L7571 was passed on to No 61 Sqn in May 1942, and was then in turn transferred to No 207 Sqn in September of that same year. Coded EM-S, and flown by Flt Sgt J D M Heron RNZAF, the bomber was lost on one of its first missions with its new unit when, on the night of 16/17 September, it failed to return from Essen. Nine Lancasters were lost from a force of 369 bombers.

16
Lancaster B I ED382/SR-J of No 101 Sqn, Holme-on-Spalding Moor, 4 May 1943

Widely regarded as an evil tyrant at the outbreak of war, Soviet leader Josef Stalin had been rapidly rehabilitated by Allied propagandists following Operation Barbarossa. This No 101 Sqn Lancaster, JOE, was named in his honour, and carried mission markings in the form of crossed Union Jacks and Russian flags. It was flown at that time by Flg Off Don Austin, and went on to serve with Nos 625 and 300 Sqns. A true survivor, ED382 spent time

with No 1 Lancaster Finishing School (LFS), No 1662 HCU and Bomber Command Instructors' School after being retired from frontline flying. Finally grounded in July 1945, the veteran bomber was duly classified as Ground Instructional Machine 5296M.

17
Lancaster B III ED905/PM-X of No 103 Sqn, Elsham Wolds, May 1943

Flt Lt Van Rolleghem's Lancaster carried crossed British and Belgian flags on the nose. Like ED382, this aircraft was destined to have a long career, later moving to No 166 Sqn (where an Indian Chief's head was added below the flags) and eventually to No 550 Sqn. Removed from the frontline in late 1944, ED905 subsequently spent time with No 1 LFS and No 1656 HCU until being written off whilst still serving with the latter unit on 20 August 1945. The weary bomber's undercarriage collapsed during a heavy landing at the HCU's Lindholme base – it had flown an incredible 628+ hours.

18
Lancaster B I R5677/ZN-A of No 106 Sqn, Coningsby, September 1942

No 106 Sqn conducted a large number of mining ('Gardening') sorties, and so had a clutch of naval officers on charge to the squadron, giving it something of a maritime air. Admiral Chattanooga was one of several aircraft with 'Admiral'-prefixed nicknames. This aircraft (wearing a non-standard roundel) was captained by a Rhodesian pilot, Flt Lt W N Whamond. He flew one of the three aircraft (R5574) sortied on the raid on Gdynia on 27/28 July 1942, and was heavily involved in the first operational drops of the new 8000-lb HC bomb. A veteran of 67 ops (and 512 flying hours), R5677 was lost on the 29/30 May 1943 raid on Wuppertal, this mission being the most successful staged by Bomber Command during the entire Battle of the Ruhr. Some 719 aircraft (including 292 Lancasters) effectively obliterated 80 per cent of the Barmen district of Wuppertal, destroying five out of six of the town's largest factories, 211 other industrial premises and nearly 4000 homes. It is estimated that approximately 3400 people were killed by the mini 'firestorm' that developed in the narrow streets of the old centre of the town. In return, Bomber Command lost 33 aircraft, including seven Lancasters.

19
Lancaster B I W4118/ZN-Y of No 106 Sqn, Syerston, November 1942

Admiral Prune was a regular mount of No 106 Sqn's charismatic leader, Wg Cdr Guy Gibson, who would later gain fame as CO of the 'Dambusters'. It was one of six aircraft modified to carry the Capital Ship Bomb – modifications which saw the central bomb-carrying beam being locally strengthened to permit the carriage of the 5600-lb weapon. The aircraft was flown by Gibson on the mission to Gdynia on 27/28 July 1942, although bomb aimer Sqn Ldr Robinson was unable to get the bomb within 400 yards of the *Gneisenau*. The aircraft was also used for early drops of the first 8000-lb HC bombs, and was sometimes flown by Sqn Ldr John de Lacy 'Dim' Wooldridge, OC B Flight. Wooldridge, the son of a distinguished RFC pilot, flew Hampdens and Manchesters with No 207 Sqn, transferring to No 106 Sqn to oversee the unit's conversion to the Lancaster, being rapidly promoted from flying officer to acting squadron leader in the process. Wooldridge led the first three 'thousand bomber' raids, and rounded off his second tour with a DFC and bar and a total of 73 operations. He subsequently flew Mosquitos. Gibson flew *Admiral Prune* on the raid against Le Creusot, during which it sustained minor damage. W4118 was lost on the Turin raid on 4/5 February 1943, by which time it had flown 340 hours. Of the 188 aircraft (77 Lancasters) sortied that night, 156 made it to Turin, where three Avro bombers were lost.

20
Lancaster B II DS685/KO-A of No 115 Sqn, Little Snoring, August 1943
With its bulged bomb doors, and short, Beaufighter-style engine air cooler intakes, DS685 was typical of many B IIs, but lacked a ventral gun turret. The aircraft was regularly flown by the CO, Wg Cdr Sims, until it was shot down over Hamburg on 2/3 August 1943. On this occasion the aircraft's commander was Sgt C Button, who led an all-NCO crew. A total of 740 aircraft (329 Lancasters) attempted to bomb Hamburg on this mission, but a large thunderstorm over Germany scattered the formation, and many crews turned back early. At least four aircraft were lost due to wing icing, turbulence or lightning strikes, and a total of 30 bombers (13 Lancasters) were posted missing. DS685 had flown just 44 hours by the time it was lost.

21
Lancaster B I W4851/GT-E of No 156 Sqn, No 8 (PFF) Group, Warboys, April 1943
Flt Lt R S D Kearns RNZAF applied a 'Saint' insignia to each of his aircraft. No 156 Sqn had been No 1 Group's contribution to the Pathfinder Force, flying Wellingtons, but had converted to Lancasters in January 1943. Kearns went on to No 617 Sqn after his tour with the Pathfinders. Because they lay outside the old-established Bomber Groups, the Pathfinder Lancaster squadrons experienced some difficulties in getting replacement aircraft, and in late 1942 and early 1943 were still operating some of the oldest and most tired B Is in frontline service. Serving briefly with No 101 Sqn following its lengthy spell with No 156 Sqn, W4851 was transferred to No 1656 HCU during the second half of 1943, and became a part of No 3 LFS upon its formation at Feltwell in December of that same year. The aircraft was lost when it collided in mid air with fellow No 3 LFS

Lancaster B I ED376 near Lakenheath on 17 June 1944. This was a sad ending for two veteran bombers, for W4851 had flown 744 hours and ED376 660 hours.

22
Lancaster B III ED905/AS-X of No 166 Sqn, Kirmington, September 1943
When No 166 Sqn formed from No 103 Sqn's 'C' Flight, Flt Lt Van Rolleghem's old mount (see profile 17) was among the aircraft transferred, exchanging its PM codes for AS, but retaining the individual letter X and the crossed Belgian and British flags. New skipper Sqn Ldr B Pape added a Red Indian chief's head motif to the nose.

23
Lancaster B I R5570/EM-F of No 207 Sqn, Bottesford, May 1942
No 207 Sqn was Bomber Command's third Lancaster unit, and was declared operational during April 1942. Having initially been issued to No 83 Sqn, R5570 subsequently became one of the first Lancasters assigned to No 207 Sqn, and was a participant in each of Bomber Command's first two 'thousand bomber' raids at the end of May 1942. The aircraft then still wore light grey unit codes, but had already been fitted with the fairing around the mid-upper turret which both restricted the field of fire (preventing the gunner from hitting parts of his own aircraft) and reduced drag. R5570 was lost on the 8/9 December 1942 raid on Turin whilst being flown by the unit's CO, Wg Cdr F G L Bain. It was the sole Lancaster to be posted missing from a force of 108 despatched (133 No 5 Group aircraft were sortied in total). R5570 had amassed 230 flying hours by the time it was shot down.

24
Lancaster B X KB700/LQ-Q of No 405 Sqn, Gransden Lodge, November 1943
KB700 was the first Canadian-built Lancaster B X, arriving in the UK in September 1943. Delivered to No 405 Sqn on 5 October, it was later transferred to No 419. Unusually, *THE RUHR EXPRESS* badge was applied on both sides of the nose. For most of its time with No 405 Sqn the aircraft was usually flown by Plt Off Harold Arthur Floren. It had been planned that the bomber would return to Canada for use selling War Bonds after its 50th operation, but the aircraft collided with a tractor on landing at Middleton St George on 2 January 1945 and was burned out.

25
Lancaster B II DS708/OW-Q of No 426 Sqn, Linton-on-Ouse, November 1943
During late 1943, the decoration of No 426 ('Thunderbird') Sqn's Lancasters was neat and relatively restrained. Much of it was applied by LAC E J Black, one of the unit's more talented engine mechanics. Q-for-Queen of No 426 Sqn carried a Queen of Hearts playing card badge on the nose.

This aircraft was fitted with bulged bomb doors, but did not have a ventral gun turret. It remained with No 426 Sqn until the unit converted to Halifax B IIIs in April-May 1944, DS708 then being transferred to No 408 Sqn (where it was coded EQ-A). It was passed on to Short Brothers of Rochester in February 1945, and eventually wound up at the Royal Aircraft Establishment at Farnborough post-war, where it conducted trials for the servo spring tab controls eventually fitted to the Bristol Brabazon airliner. DS708 ended its days as a target on the bombing range at Foulness in 1950.

26
Lancaster B II DS689/OW-S of No 426 Sqn, Linton-on-Ouse, September 1943
No 426 Sqn was chosen as a Lancaster B II unit because its air- and groundcrew already had extensive experience of operating radial-engined Wellingtons. Converting to the new type in June 1943, the unit kept its Lancasters for just over a year, trading them for radial-engined Halifaxes in April-May 1944. This particular aircraft was one of four Lancasters lost (from a force of 343 sortied) on the 7/8 October 1943 raid on Stuttgart.

27
Lancaster B III JB607/AR-N of No 460 Sqn, Binbrook, Winter 1943
JB607 was one of the first H_2S-equipped Lancasters, and wore No 460 Sqn's later AR code prefix in place of the UV codes originally used on the unit's Lancasters. No 460 Sqn had stood down from ops with Wellingtons in September 1942, and began to convert to Halifaxes, but before it could recommence operations, it started to receive Lancasters instead. JB607, flown by Plt Off S J Ireland RAAF, failed to return from a mission to Berlin on 29/30 December 1943. Some 457 Lancasters (from a total force of 712 aircraft) attacked the German capital that night, and 11 Avro bombers were lost.

28
Lancaster B III ED539/PO-V of No 467 Sqn, Bottesford, Summer 1943
Another RAAF Lancaster unit was No 467 Sqn. Issued to the unit in late January 1943, ED539 boasted a 56-mission bomb log, augmented by medal ribbons and a badge combining the aircraft's individual code letter with a Kookaburra dangling Hitler's head from its beak, come the summer of that same year. The aircraft was captained by Plt Off Bill Manifold RAAF for much of 1943. ED539 was lost on the 27/28 January 1944 mission to Berlin, the force of 515 Lancasters despatched being mauled by German nightfighters – 33 bombers were posted missing.

29
Lancaster B IS ED912/G/AJ-S of No 617 Sqn, Coningsby, December 1943
ED912/G flew on the 'Dams Raid' as AJ-N, skippered by Flt Lt Knight. By December the code

had changed to AJ-S, and ownership had passed to Flt Lt R S D Kearns, who had the aircraft decorated with a flamboyant winged saint figure. Interestingly, this B IS still retained its cutaway bomb bay and *Upkeep* mounting arms. Remaining in service with No 617 Sqn into 1945, ED912/G was eventually placed in storage with No 46 Maintenance Unit in February of that year and Struck off Charge and sold for scrap on 26 September 1946.

30
Lancaster B X CF-CMS (ex-B I R5727), Canadian TransAtlantic Air Service, late 1943
Ex-No 44 Sqn machine R5727 was flown to Canada on 25 August 1942 as a fully-armed B I, complete with a ventral gun turret. After use as the pattern aircraft for Canadian B X production, the bomber was delivered to Victory Aircraft for conversion to transport configuration, and registered CF-CMS. It commenced flying the transatlantic route between Montreal (Dorval) and Prestwick, in Scotland, in July 1943. This aircraft also reportedly served as an engine test-bed with Rolls-Royce in mid 1942.

BIBLIOGRAPHY

HOLMES, HARRY, *Avro Lancaster, The Definitive Record*. Airlife, 1997

MASON, FRANCIS K, *The Avro Lancaster*. Aston, 1989

MASON, FRANCIS K, *Major Archive Avro Lancaster Bs I-III*. Cerberus/Container, undated

FRANKS, RICHARD A, *The Avro Lancaster, Manchester and Lincoln (Modellers Datafile No 4)*. SAM Publications, 2000

FLYPAST SPECIAL, *Lancaster, A Tribute to Britain's Most Famous Bomber*. Key, 1998

MACKAY, R S G, *Lancaster, in Action*. Squadron/Signal, 1982

BUSHELL, SUE J, *Avro Lancaster, Mighty Hero of the Night Sky*. Maze Media, 1996

GARBETT, MIKE AND GOULDING, BRIAN, *The Lancaster At War*. Ian Allan, 1971

GARBETT, MIKE AND GOULDING, BRIAN, *The Lancaster At War 2*. Ian Allan, 1979

GARBETT, MIKE AND GOULDING, BRIAN, *The Lancaster At War 3*. Ian Allan, 1984

GARBETT, MIKE AND GOULDING, BRIAN, *The Lancaster At War 4 - Pathfinder Squadrons*. Ian Allan, 1990

GARBETT, MIKE AND GOULDING, BRIAN, *The Lancaster At War 5 - Fifty Years On*. Ian Allan, 1995

GARBETT, MIKE AND GOULDING, BRIAN, *Avro Lancaster I, Profile No 65*. Profile Publications, undated.

ROBERTSON, BRUCE, *Avro Lancaster II, Profile No 235*. Profile Publications, undated.

GARBETT, MIKE AND GOULDING, BRIAN, *Avro Lancaster in Unit Service*. Osprey Aircam No 12, 1968

PATTERSON, DAN AND DICK, RON, *Lancaster RAF Heavy Bomber*. Airlife, 1996

GOULDING, BRIAN, GARBETT, MIKE AND PARTRIDGE, JOHN, *Story of a Lanc*. Lincolnshire Aviation Heritage Centre, 1991

JACKSON, A J, *Avro Aircraft Since 1908*. Putnam, 1990

THETFORD, OWEN, *Aircraft of the Royal Air Force since 1918*. Putnam, 1995

BOWYER, MICHAEL J F, *Aircraft for the Many*. PSL, 1995

BOWYER, MICHAEL J F, *Bombing Colours, RAF Bombers, their markings and operations, 1937-73*. PSL, 1973

FOCHUK, STEPHEN M, *Metal Canvas, Canadians and World War II Aircraft Nose Art*. Vanwell/Canadian War Museum, 1999

HMSO, *Bomber Command*.

HMSO, *Bomber Command Continues*. 1943

HASTINGS, MAX, *Bomber Command*. Michael Joseph,1979

OVERY, RICHARD *Bomber Command 1939-45*. HarperCollins, 1997

TERRAINE, JOHN, *The Right of the Line*. Hodder, 1985

HARVEY, MAURICE, *The Allied Bomber War, 1939-1945*. Spellmount, 1992

FREEMAN, ROGER A, *Raiding the Reich*. Arms & Armour Press, 1997

DELVE, KEN, AND JACOBS, PETER, *The Six Year Offensive*. Arms & Armour Press, 1992

BOWYER, CHAZ, *Bomber Barons*. Kimber, 1983

BOWYER, CHAZ, *For Valour*. Grub St, 1992

TURNER, JOHN FRAYN, *VCs of the Air*. Airlife, 1993

MOYES, PHILIP, *Bomber Squadrons of the RAF and their Aircraft*. MacDonald, 1964 and 1976

HALLEY, JAMES J, *The Squadrons of the Royal Air Force*. Air-Britain Publications.

JEFFORD Wg Cdr C G, *RAF Squadrons*. Airlife, 1988

DELVE, KEN, *The Source Book of the RAF*. Airlife, 1994

STURTIVANT et al, *Royal Air Force Flying Training and Support Units*. Air-Britain, 1998

BIDDLE, TAMI DAVIS, 'British and American Approaches to Strategic Bombing', published in *Air Power in Theory and Practise by John Gooch*. Cass, 1995

PARKS, W HAYS, 'Precision and Area Bombing – who did which, and when?', published in *Air Power in Theory and Practise by John Gooch*. Cass, 1995

BENNETT, AVM D C T, *Pathfinder*. Frederick Muller, 1958

GIBSON, E M, *Enemy Coast Ahead*. Michael Joseph,1946

INDEX

References to illustrations are shown in **bold**. Plates are shown with page and caption locators in (brackets).